OTABIND®

INTERNATIONAL

Dear Friend:

You may have noticed that this book is put together differently than most other quality paperbacks. The page you are reading, for instance, along with the back page, is glued to the cover. And when you open the book the spine "floats" in back of the pages. But there's nothing wrong with your book. These features allow us to produce what is known as a detached cover, specifically designed to prevent the spine from cracking even after repeated use. A state-of-the-art binding technology known as OtaBind® is used in the manufacturing of this and all Health Communications, Inc. books.

HCI has invested in equipment and resources that ensure the books we produce are of the highest quality, yet remain affordable. At our Deerfield Beach headquarters, our editorial and art departments are just a few steps from our pressroom, bindery and shipping facilities. This internal production enables us to pay special attention to the needs of our readers when we create our books.

Our titles are w
quality of your life
ring to this book
to share it with fa
benefit from the
these reasons, ou

D0813151

and, more importantly, user-friendly.

OtaBind® gives us these qualities. Along with a crease-free spine, the book you have in your hands has some other characteristics you may not be aware of:

- Open the book to any page and it will lie flat, so you'll never have to worry about losing your place.

- You can bend the book over backwards without damage, allowing you to hold it with one hand.

- The spine is 3-5 times stronger than conventional perfect binding, preventing damage even with rough handling.

This all adds up to a better product for our readers—one that will last for years to come. We stand behind the quality of our books and guarantee that, if you're not completely satisfied, we'll replace the book or refund your money within 30 days of purchase. If you have any questions about this guarantee or our bookbinding process, please feel free to contact our customer service department at 1-800-851-9100.

We hope you enjoy the quality of this book, and find understanding, insight and direction for your life in the information it provides.

Health Communications, Inc.®

3201 S.W. 15th Street
Deerfield Beach, FL 33442-8190
(305) 360-0909

Peter Vegso
President

RECLAIMING PRIDE

RECLAIMING PRIDE

Daily Reflections On Gay
And Lesbian Life

....

Joseph H. Neisen, Ph.D.

Health Communications, Inc.
Deerfield Beach, Florida

©1994 Joseph H. Neisen, P.h.D.
ISBN 1-55874-312-X

Publisher: Health Communications, Inc.
             3201 S.W. 15th Street
             Deerfield Beach, Florida 33442-8190

This book is dedicated to my godson and nephew, Troy, in the belief that the next generation will be more loving, caring and accepting of lesbians and gays and afford us the respect we, as all people, deserve.

PREFACE

Our struggle for social justice and the basic human and legal rights we are all entitled to has become increasingly visible in the 25 years since Stonewall. It is relatively easy to measure our progress in terms of notable milestones because there have been many—a million-plus marchers in Washington, passage of supportive legislation in many cities and states, election and appointment of gays and lesbians to public office and victories in the courts. It is impossible to know or recount all of the untold acts of individual honesty, courage and sometimes defiance that have now made our presence inescapable in families, churches, workplaces, the arts, sports and politics.

It is in the power of these individual actions, more than all of the marches, legislation and court decisions, that the seeds of true respect and understanding, or at the very least acceptance, find their most fertile ground. Gays and lesbians who have come out of the closet can usually associate their initial open declaration of sexuality with such an action—an acknowledgment to a friend or a talk with parents. And this individual action is accompanied by a realization that it is only the first in a continuous progression of steps that can affirm and strengthen our gay and lesbian identity.

Despite that realization, and despite all of our recent successes, we live in a world where gays and lesbians remain objects of hate, discrimination and even physical harm. In this world, it is still sometimes easier to choose the well-worn path of least resistance and perceived security. Consequently, that first step may never be followed by the second or third or the hundredth step. For some, there may never even be a first.

To ensure otherwise, we must regularly build on our sense of dignity and self-esteem. We must celebrate our heroes, our rich history and the breadth of our accomplishments and contributions in the face of much adversity. We must recognize the injustice that springs from bigotry and intolerance. And most of all, we must comprehend the terrible cost of silence, of deception, of life in the closet, of fear of ourselves. When we have done all this, those steps are no longer as difficult and the power of our actions, as individuals, can bring the change that we all seek.

Gregg Larson
Minneapolis/St. Paul

Our sexuality is an indivisible aspect of our humanity. To ask us, regardless of our sexual orientation, to deny and reject our sexuality—who we fantasize about, who we desire, who we fall in love with, who we love—is to ask us to split ourselves away from the most fundamental part of our being, the place which is at the center of our humanity, from which all longing, desire, passion and creativity emerges.

For all of us whose sexuality does not "fit" society's suffocated definition of what is acceptable, it is important to recognize that the forces which strangle and repress our sexuality are powerful and they are embedded in our nation's psyche. Lesbian, gay, bisexual and transgender individuals have become the scapegoats of a sex-phobic society that projects the results of its most profound torment onto us.

To "come out," to emerge from under the layers of societal confusion and hatred, we need anchors—words and images that we can grasp onto, that tell us of our beauty, our courage and the opportunities present through our oppression. These opportunities are to be free of the shackles of societal expectations, to develop a sensitive ear to hear our own creative voices as well as others' and to have the courage to follow our dreams individually and collectively.

This book is an anchor. It is a gift to all of us who struggle to maintain our integrity and our humanity. It is an antidote to shame, a message of love and hope, a voice reaching out every day to quiet our fears and reduce our isolation. Ultimately, this book is an invitation to move beyond tolerance and acceptance to a celebration of our individuality as well as our connections to one another as expressed through a deeply creative force, our sexuality.

Françoise Susset
Montreal, Canada

INTRODUCTION

··

This book was written for several reasons. First, to provide hope and encouragement for those lesbians and gays in the early stages of their coming out process. Lesbians and gays frequently struggle with accepting and valuing their homosexuality because of the heterosexism and homophobia still rampant in our society. This book is primarily for these individuals. Second, this book is to provide a reminder to those of us who have been out for years, that coming out never stops. There is always a next step, and we have a responsibility to be positive role models for those individuals still struggling with self-acceptance. It is important to remember that they would not be struggling if lesbians and gays were accepted and respected in the first place. Lastly, this book was written so that heterosexuals might learn more about us and recognize that we will no longer be silenced.

In some ways this book is a bit of a "manifesto" in that the daily reflections are a call for personal action, coming out, reclaiming pride and personal empowerment. In this regard, you might refer to the writings as "The Little Lavender Book." Be proud . . . and raise your voice!

The quotations used in this book are either by lesbians and gays, about lesbians and gays, or simply related to our struggles. They are from well-known voices in our communities, and lesser-known voices. Though they are not representative of all our voices, they will hopefully convey the message that each of us has a voice that deserves to be heard.

A special thanks goes to several dear friends. To Françoise Susset and Gregg Larson, who offer the preface, with whom I have shared many discussions regarding lesbian and gay issues and the need for lesbians and gays to be visible, assertive and proud. To Don Donahugh for lending his ideas for the cover. And, to Sheryl Griffin, who once again has assisted me in preparing manuscripts for publication; Sheryl embodies the accepting nonchalant attitude we deserve from all heterosexuals!

Our visions begin with our desires.

Audre Lorde
writer

As we reflect back on the past it becomes more clear how the shaming messages about homosexuality contribute to the development of a negative self-image and lack of hope for the future. It is true—oppression squelches desires and passions. Anti-gay bigotry often keeps lesbians and gays from pursuing their dreams and goals. The dreams may be so buried that we lose sight of what they were.

As the new year begins take time to find your dreams. Rediscover your desires and passions. They are inside waiting to be rekindled and realized!

We will not change the world until we change ourselves.

Tim McFeeley
executive director
Human Rights Campaign Fund

We are only beginning to realize the pervasiveness of the victimization we have suffered. Yes, we recognize the obvious painful effects. And yes, our actions have brought many changes in the last two decades. Yet our lingering shame keeps us from making more changes. Our sporadic lapses into silence are vestiges of shame.

We must continue to unleash each and every layer of shame that we once believed was already unleashed. As we do so, even more change is possible.

I don't think there is a more powerful advocate than a parent.

Paulette Goodman
past president
Federation of Parents and Friends
of Lesbians and Gays (PFLAG)

Our families can do a great deal to foster acceptance of lesbians and gays. But first, we must come out to our families. Next, we can support our families in their coming out process. And after our families reach a place of acceptance, we can challenge them to do more—to stand up and speak out for their gay family member(s).

Just as our visibility helps generate acceptance, our families need to come out of the closet. Their visibility can help others see we are all family.

Ask a family member to stand up for you. You deserve it!

It's far harder to kill a phantom than a reality.

Virginia Woolf
writer

Remember coming out to Mom or Dad or a friend? Their reply being, "You know, that's okay!" And it seemed as if they were more accepting of your homosexuality than maybe you were? It happens. Even with the approval of others we can still struggle with self-acceptance. It's a reminder that the shaming messages that we grew up with are still powerful. It also tells us that our self-esteem must be fostered from within.

Validation from others is limited when we do not validate ourselves. Release the shame. Affirm your homosexuality.

❀

Gay, Lesbian, Bi and Straight, we are the community and family of God, and we are here knowing that God loves us.

Reverend Nathan Baxter
dean
National Cathedral of Washington

What an affirmation of lesbians, gays and bisexuals! Too often when we hear the words lesbian and gay in church the message is hate, not affirmation. Consider the importance of Reverend Baxter's affirmation from the National Cathedral. The message is clear: We are all family. All sexual orientations are equally valued.

It is time for people of all sexual orientations to join hands together. Whose hand can you reach out to today?

"Hope" is the thing with feathers—
That perches in the soul—
And sings the tune without the words—
And never stops—at all.

Emily Dickinson
poet

Prejudice and discrimination can bury hope. Prejudice and discrimination can also fuel anger and indignation that keep hope alive. A victim becomes a pessimist. A survivor maintains hope. Hope lives inside each of us in spite of the prejudices we have faced as lesbians and gays.

Keep hope alive. Be a survivor!

Never underestimate the power of pride.

T-shirt slogan

Sometimes it may seem that affirmations and reclaiming pride do no good. The power of affirmations is seen more clearly over time. It may be that beginning to claim your pride as a lesbian/gay individual seems phoney. Of course that's often the case, considering all the shaming messages we grew up with. However, each affirmation is a step in reclaiming our pride. Each time we say "Gay and Proud," we heal.

Give yourself time. After months and years of affirmation, you will see the power of pride.

If God dislikes gays so much, how come he picked Michelangelo, a known homosexual, to paint the Sistine Chapel ceiling while assigning Anita [Bryant] to go on TV and push orange juice.

Mike Royko
Chicago columnist

When we look at homosexuality through-out history, we realize we have much to be proud of. Of course, as we were growing up, most of us didn't hear about the contributions made by homosexuals. Instead we heard an overabundance of myths and stereotypes perpetuated by people like Anita.

Look around. Re-examine history. How refreshing to finally reclaim our rightful place in history!

The wave of the future is coming and there is no stopping it.

Anne Morrow Lindbergh
writer

Years of prejudice and discrimination can leave us feeling like change is not possible. However, change is certain. Change is constant.

Are you holding back on change? Are you doing what you can do to make sure whatever changes will occur are positive? You can flow with the wave and take your chances, or create a wave and ensure positive change.

The enemy is everyone, gay or straight, who passively supports oppression by their silence.

Romanovsky & Phillips
singers/songwriters

We do desperately want straight people to speak up for our rights, and rightly so. But we must ask ourselves if we are doing what we can do at the moment to create a world tolerant of lesbians and gays. Are there times we hear fag jokes and don't respond when we know we are capable of doing so? Are we complacent at work about staying in the closet when we know our co-workers already know and are accepting?

Our silence hurts us. There's always a next step in speaking up. Next time, go for it!

When one has been threatened with a great injustice, one accepts a smaller as a favor.

Jane Welsh Carlyle

Lesbians and gays are sometimes grateful for "smaller injustices" against us rather than "larger injustices" so that we lose the bigger picture. Any kind of injustice is wrong.

Stopping oppression is not a favor. It's the only moral thing to do. Victims accept what is given to them. Be a survivor, demand no further injustices.

Wouldn't it be great if you could only get AIDS from giving money to television preachers?

Elayne Boosler
comedian

"AIDS is a punishment from God for being gay." How many times have we heard this from religious fanatics? How do they explain all the heterosexuals with AIDS? It doesn't take much to recognize the bigotry clouded in religiosity.

Yet, sometimes when we are feeling vulnerable or when we haven't realized all the shaming messages about being gay that we heard growing up, we might actually buy into that stuff about AIDS as a punishment. Don't let the loud voices of bigotry re-trigger your shame. AIDS provides each of us an opportunity to point out the bigotry and to let go of our shame.

Dare to dream.

Anonymous

One day I was working with a gay man, a rancher from out West. He knew he was gay since his teenage years, but now in his 50s he was just getting involved with the gay community. Though a whole new world was open to him, the years of silence fostered fear and trepidation. He reveled in the companionship and comfort of his new friends, but because of the newness of it all saw few options for himself.

Dare to dream . . . a reminder for all of us as we face coming out further and further. We can make our dreams happen.

Why do dykes have 500 ways to save the earth when most ordinary mortals have only 50?

Susie Bright
author

Gifted and gay! Say it over and over. We are courageous. We are innovative. We are caring, loving and compassionate. We have special gifts.

Look around and take note. Celebrate our gifts!

Justice denied anywhere diminishes justice everywhere.

Martin Luther King, Jr.

The NAACP (National Association for the Advancement of Colored People) endorsed the 1993 March on Washington for Lesbian, Gay and Bi Equal Rights and Liberation. Speaking at the march, representatives from the NAACP emphasized the importance of freedom and justice for *all* people. Though others clamor that our struggles are different, the NAACP endorsement is a clear message that we must join hands in the fight for justice.

Let each of us re-examine our biases. Remember, our struggle is part of a larger struggle for justice, respect and dignity.

When I dream I am always ageless.

Elizabeth Coatsworth

When we lose our dreams, we stop growing and start dying. The prejudices we have faced because we are gay have resulted in many of us losing sight of our dreams.

To live, to grow, to be . . . we must rekindle our dreams. These dreams are likely to be tied to coming out and being true to ourselves. Being true to ourselves is the first and only necessary ingredient in realizing our dreams.

Nature never repeats herself, and the possibilities of one human soul will never be found in another.

Elizabeth Cady Stanton

Each of us has unique gifts and talents. Years of prejudice and discrimination fuel low self-esteem causing us to lose sight of our gifts, strengths and talents.

Take time to re-examine and search inside yourself. Rediscover your gifts and use them. You have something to offer that no one else can.

Coming out is no longer the sum total of our strategy; we are about power.

John D'Emilio
gay historian

Coming out is a precursor of power. As individuals we regain our personal power by coming out. As a community, our power multiplies as more individuals come out. With increasing numbers of lesbians and gays coming out to family, friends and co-workers, we have secured power as a community.

This power was created from a base of individual acts of courage. Remember that our personal courageous acts are the life force that established and maintains our community's power.

I would like to believe when I die that I have given myself away like a tree that sows seed every Spring and never counts the loss, because it is not loss, it is adding to future life.

May Sarton
poet

When you reflect on your life, consider whether, like a tree, you have matured to produce the seeds for new life. Some young trees die before spring. As individuals, we sometimes stay stuck and question whether our life and labors will bear any fruits or whether we have left our mark for future generations. Much of this questioning is tied to whether or not we come out or how far out of the closet we actually step.

Continue to grow like the tree. What seeds will you leave for the next generation of lesbians and gays?

I started doing public speaking at high schools, which wasn't easy because I was called a faggot all through high school. It's been good, though. One reason I do it is because I don't want to die in obscurity.

Jonathan Brown

Facing the fears and the pains aids healing because it produces self-confidence and pride. We may still be saddened and in pain by the memories, but the memories no longer rule our lives.

In our own time, we can and do transform the memories from something painful to something that now gives strength and courage. Hearing "faggots" no longer triggers shame, but produces anger and sadness toward those who spew such hatred. Hearing "faggots," instead, becomes a call to strengthen our pride.

Male and female represent two sides of the great radical dualism. But in fact they are perpetually passing into one another. Fluid hardens to solid, solid rushes to fluid. There is no wholly masculine man, no purely feminine woman.

Margaret Fuller

Those people who espouse traditional male and female roles are those who have the most difficulty accepting homosexuality. They are threatened by anything that does not adhere to a strict code of male power and female subordination. Hence, the connection between sexism and heterosexism.

Lesbians and gays take pride as our voices challenge these harmful stereotypes! We no longer have to deny our masculine or feminine side. Celebrate both the masculine and feminine within yourself.

We are entitled to personal anger, as well as retribution for crimes committed against us. Feeling this way should not be cause for violence against us, nor guilt for speaking out.

Patricia Cumbie
editor

The anger lesbians and gays feel is righteous anger. Slowly we are gaining retribution for the crimes committed against us because we are gay. As we express our anger, however, there is a vocal minority that raises their voice to further oppress us because they do not believe we have the right to speak up. We must not feel guilty for speaking up. Individuals who have been victimized tend to shy away under such circumstances.

To be a survivor is to refuse to let others make us feel guilty and to continue to voice our hurt and anger.

The importance of the 1993 March on Washington is the energy that it gives to participants.

Barney Frank
representative from Massachusetts

A community gathered together fosters personal pride as we come to realize we are not alone. Community is power. Family is power. With them comes pride. Pride and personal power go hand in hand.

Reclaim your pride by reaching out and participating in your community. The community provides healing. The community offers the potential for personal transformation.

We're shattering centuries of silence by being open as gay people.

Urvasha Vaid
former executive director
National Lesbian and Gay Task Force (NLGTF)

Centuries of silence have compelled us to speak up. Oppression silences people . . . temporarily. However, as the oppression endures, the need to speak up multiplies because the pain of the oppression becomes unbearable. When one voice speaks of the pain, a litany of others follows. For there is little left to lose, but much to be gained—for this sharing provides healing, it soothes the wounds. The wounds heal and we will no longer be silent.

The fact is that more people have been slaughtered in the name of religion than for any other single reason. That, my friends, that is true perversion!

Harvey Milk
former San Francisco city supervisor

Hatred is perversion. Homosexuality is not.

Bigotry is perversion. Lesbians and gays are not.

To classify homosexuality as a perversion in the name of religiosity, is the ultimate perversion. Homosexuality is not a religious issue. Homosexuality is reality.

Religious zealots try to make homosexuality a nonentity even though it is a fact of life. When religious zealots try to cloud the issues, keep it simple and keep it clear: Homosexuality is just fine, but bigotry and hatred have got to go.

Homophobia is insecurity about being heterosexual.

T-shirt slogan

We have grown up with false messages that homosexuality is sick, evil, wrong, sinful and immoral. When we reach the point of recognizing these lies, it becomes much clearer how our society has such difficulty dealing with sexuality in general, and homosexuality even more. Messages about homosexuality being sick and evil are not just the voice of someone who is misinformed, but someone who has a lot of personal hang-ups.

Society is just beginning to realize that homosexuality is not a mental illness. Perhaps prejudice and insecurity are the real signs of emotional problems.

Happiness is the state of consciousness which proceeds from the achievement of one's values.

Ayn Rand
writer

Healing from the shaming messages about lesbians and gays we grew up with means that we need to learn to value being lesbian and gay. Valuing being gay and lesbian is something that should have been taught but was not.

It is absurd to expect children to value themselves when an intrinsic and inseparable part of our being, our homosexuality, is denied. So, we must go about putting back together the whole, incorporating our homosexuality into what we value about ourselves. As we join together all parts of the self, we release the shame from the past and we embrace and celebrate our lives. This in turn teaches others to value their sexuality as an integral part of life.

The greatest cause of psychopathology in the young is the unlived lives of their parents.

Carl Jung
psychologist

A gay friend who had married, had children and then come out of the closet shared this quote with me. He talked about staying in the marriage and in the closet because he loved his children and didn't want to hurt them. After years, he realized that staying in the closet was not only a tremendous emotional cost to himself, but to his children also.

When we hide our lives, our children don't get to know who we really are. They only know a shell that ultimately provides limited love and support. And, on some level, they already know we are lesbian or gay. There is still time to share your life with those you love.

[Michael in "The Boys in the Band"]: *The Christ-was-I-drunk-last-night syndrome. You know, when you made it with some guy in school and the next day when you had to face each other there was always a lot of . . . crap about, "Man, was I drunk last night! Christ, I don't remember a thing!"*

Mart Crowley
playwright

Our shame develops from the heterosexist messages we grew up with. Sometimes our shame manifests itself in self-destructive behaviors like excessive drinking or drugging. Our shame may be so entrenched that the only way we think we can "express our homosexuality" is when we are drunk or high.

Excessive drinking and drugging prevent us from developing a positive self-image. Affirming our homosexuality may be necessary to stop alcohol and drug abuse. Take time to examine the connection between any self-destructive behaviors and lingering shame.

We shall hardly notice in a year or two. You can get accustomed to anything.

Edna St. Vincent Millay
poet

As children, initially we are tremendously uncomfortable with all the anti-gay messages, both overt and covert. Because we lack support at this stage of life we develop a protective defense mechanism and become "accustomed" to these shaming messages. When we grow up we then fear coming out, and we fear change because this false sense of "comfortability" is so ingrained.

As we struggle with furthering our coming out process, we need to remind ourselves that we will become comfortable "out." And this will not be a false comfort, but a comfort that will grow strong, nurture and heal.

If the Berlin Wall can come down, so can the wall keeping gays and lesbians as outlaws.

Phyllis Burke
author

Keep hope alive. We live in a world where the impossible does happen. Just 25 years ago homosexuality was not discussed; lesbian and gay civil rights was unheard of.

Today, we are visible, and it is only a matter of time before we will have full civil rights. Victims often give up hope. Survivors keep hope alive.

We must be proud of who we are, and we cannot do that when we hide.

Martina Navratilova
professional tennis player

The message is consistent. The message is clear. To reclaim our personal pride we must come out. This theme is heard with increasing frequency.

Coming out is a lifelong process, not a one-time event. There is always another step. Take that next step today. Each step you take is a step in reclaiming pride, your own personal pride.

We maintain that we have the right to exist after the fashion which nature made us. And if we cannot alter your laws, we shall go on breaking them. You may condemn us to infamy, exile, prison—as you formerly burned witches. You may degrade our emotional instincts and drive us into vice and misery. But you will not eradicate inverted sexuality [homosexuality].

John Addington Symonds
Victorian writer

The same message continues from generation to generation. Homosexuality is here to stay. It always has been and always will be. We will keep on saying it until they finally "get it!"

I guess some people are just slow learners. Until they "catch up," keep in mind that once you have reclaimed your pride they cannot take it away from you even with their messages of hate. Pride is resilient.

Are homosexuals social outcasts? My God. Christopher Isherwood, Howard Brown, Merle Miller, Sidney Abbott, John Maynard Keynes. Are these people social outcasts? Some of the most moral men I know are homosexuals.

Evelyn Hooker
psychologist

The misinformed and bigoted condemn homosexuality as immoral. For heterosexuals to think they are moral and homosexuals immoral is a convenient way to justify their prejudices, while scapegoating homosexuals simply for existing. Sexual orientation does not produce "morality."

The bigger questions for everyone include: how do we live our lives? What contribution do we leave the world? Have we offered a message of hate, or a message of love and understanding?

*We must destroy the myths once and for all
. . . and most importantly, every gay person
must come out. Once they realize that we
are indeed their children, and we are indeed
everywhere, every myth, and every lie and
every innuendo will be destroyed once and
for all.*

Harvey Milk
former San Francisco city supervisor

Gay rights are human rights. Often, they are
not perceived as human rights because some
people still see lesbians and gays as subhu-
man. When we are in the closet we help perpetuate this stereotype.

Coming out helps others see us as real live
human beings. Then it becomes more clear
that we are not asking for special rights, simply human rights that all people deserve.

I am no longer willing to enter into a debate about the morality of sexual orientation, be that mine, or yours, or anyone's. Sexual orientation is not a moral issue, and so there is simply nothing to debate.

Cathy Ann Beaty
church co-pastor

Lesbian and gay people have always existed and always will. As our visibility has increased others have attempted to make homosexuality a moral issue. It is not a moral issue. Homosexuality is reality. Attempts to make it a moral issue are founded in the false hope that homosexuality will just go away.

Each time we come out we take one brick out of the wall that keeps others from seeing reality . . . from seeing us.

[On finding out he was HIV+ at age 19]: *I think the church and the schools are helping to kill young people by forcing them to stay in the closet. You're safer if you're out and in the gay community where you're exposed to information.*

Johnnie Norway

To grow and mature we need information and support. Society is still reluctant to provide us with accurate information about sex and homosexuality as we're growing up. It makes it very difficult for us to get to know ourselves. And without knowing ourselves, we cannot fully love ourselves.

Our demands for inclusion of accurate information about lesbians and gays will continue. Not because we are trying to "force our lifestyle" on others, but because we are trying to give all children the opportunity to know and love themselves.

The women I worked with took me to a lesbian club. I saw wall-to-wall women and thought, This is it! This is it! I'm in heaven! The light went on: I decided to stop lying and come out.

Dr. Zandra Rolon

After years of denying our sexuality and attempts to conform to society's expectations to be heterosexual, when we finally come out to ourselves, it is a new found freedom.

Meeting other lesbians and gays is often the catalyst that opens the door to the world we have been looking for. We can come out because we realize we are no longer alone.

[at the 1993 March on Washington]: *Liberty and justice for all. What part of* all *don't people understand?*

Patricia Schroeder
representative, U.S. House

It's not a difficult concept to grasp. Yet people's fears, insecurities, desires to control and prejudices keep them from embracing such a simple concept as justice for *all*.

How can we help others to recognize that we are part of "all"? We start by accepting ourselves for who we are. We demonstrate that we accept and celebrate diversity within our own community. We come out to family, friends, clergy and co-workers so they can no longer deny that we are, indeed, everywhere. We continue to demand equal rights until they are won. What's your next step?

Courage is the price that life exacts for granting peace.

Amelia Earhart
aviator

It takes courage to come out. We must each look within, find that courage and continue to come out to ourselves and others because there is no peace in the closet.

Internal peace and self-confidence grow with each act of coming out. Peace and self-confidence go hand in hand. They are necessary ingredients of pride.

To be calm and confident, we must each nurture and solidify our pride.

Living in a state of psychic unrest is a Borderland [and] is what makes poets write and artists create.

Gloria Anzaldua
writer

We can transform the pain that comes from living in a hostile society into something creative, powerful and beautiful.

The pain may initially leave us immobilized. However, to stay immobilized is to give up. We must transform the pain in order to survive. Then, eventually the transformation moves from surviving to thriving.

What have you done with your pain? Transform it into a positive force in your life.

Every poll shows that American voters who know a family member, loved one or someone close to them that is lesbian, gay or bisexual, support federal protection against discrimination on the basis of sexual orientation. Coming out to people who love and respect you is the most important political act you can do.

Tim McFeeley
executive director
Human Rights Campaign Fund

What is your next step in coming out? Is it no longer denying you are gay to co-workers? Talking to an aunt or uncle about being gay? Or more completely accepting your own homosexuality?

Whatever you choose, take the step today. It's more than a political act, it's part of your personal healing.

I am 15 and my girlfriend of five months is 14. I am happy. I am young. I am an honor-roll student who baby-sits the neighbors' kids. I am a lesbian.

Sarah Daniels
in a letter to the editor

There are young, bright lesbians and gay voices proclaiming their pride, refusing to buy into the shaming messages about homosexuality. This is the age of gay pride.

Have you reclaimed your pride? Young voices are reminding us that if they can . . . we all can. Proclaim your pride now!

[Regarding her custody battle to care for her partner, Sharon Kowalski, disabled in a car accident. Sharon and Karen were in the closet at the time. The courts and Sharon's parents refused to believe they were a couple. Sharon's parents were initially given guardianship.] *I spent eight years fighting for Sharon's right to speak for herself. As long as we are invisible, we are vulnerable.*

Karen Thompson

With the prejudices lesbian and gay couples face, we sometimes fail to take the steps to protect our relationships. Being out is certainly one way to do so but more is needed.

Do you have a living will? Have you checked with lesbian and gay legal experts to review your options?

Take time to protect your relationships. It's an affirmation about your life. It is an expression of your love.

Love is a basic human right.

Amnesty International

Openly sharing our love with partners and friends is something we ought to be able to take for granted. Yet there are still people who want to deny us our right to love. Fear and bigotry may spur others to try to stop us from loving. In spite of this, many lesbians and gays continue to openly express their care and love for their children and lovers. To scorn love and caring in a world that needs love is abominable.

Don't let others' bigotry keep you from love. Express your love. It is a basic human right. It is a basic human need.

Love is never a crime.

Michael Callen
AIDS activist and singer/songwriter

Because of society's fear of sex, particularly sex between two women or two men, many people lose sight of our loving relationships. The focus becomes sex, not love. And then, one form of love, heterosexual love, becomes the norm, and homosexual love becomes a crime.

To consider love, any kind of love, a crime, is absurd. Celebrate the love you have for others! It is nothing to be ashamed of or feared.

The key is that I take risks. I risk being vulnerable. I risk sharing the secrets of my heart. We already know what the straight people feel in their hearts. But no one talks about how the lesbian or gay person feels in his or her heart.

Kathleen Boatwright
vice president
Integrity (gay and lesbian Episcopalians)

Healing involves risks. Regaining our pride takes risks. We can share the secrets in our hearts. As lesbians and gays we are verbalizing the secrets in our hearts.

Let your voice be heard. Healing cannot happen in silence. Take a risk today!

Gay people have always had humor . . . looking from the fringes at heterosexuality and gender roles and heightening it to show its ridiculousness. Humor is a way in.

David Drake
actor

As much as we are justified in our anger, we must make time for humor. Sometimes our pain and anger may become so fully encompassing that we fail to recognize that all anger and no fun is detrimental to our personal healing.

Sometimes people who have been victimized don't know how to lighten up and have fun. Take time for some fun. It's good for you. And it helps straight people "get over it."

I am going forth to help repair devastations of many generations. The long dark night of my soul has passed; the days of my mourning have ended. I have stepped forth, at last, into a morning of joy.

Mary Borhek
parent of gay son

Part of our coming out is grieving the loss of heterosexual privilege. Because of the continual discrimination of lesbians and gays, the joy of coming out may be initially bittersweet.

Our anger and sadness must be vented. Expressing and releasing the anger, then, no longer interferes with taking pride in our homosexuality. Anger without pride can be self-destructive. Our pride and anger can co-exist.

Straight America is waking up to the fact that its culture is not monolithic.

Robin Stevens
writer

As children, most of us grew up with only a white, male, heterosexual perspective on history. That's all we read in junior high and high school textbooks.

Then, the women and black civil rights movements challenged America to begin to re-examine this singular historical perspective. It's taken hundreds of years to begin to re-write history so that it is more inclusive of the contributions of all people.

The chapter on the contributions of lesbians and gays has only recently begun to be written by our community.

Reclaim our place in history and reclaim your pride.

This is a society that does tragic things, obscene things; yet it is only the physical relations between human beings—the sexual relations—that we seem to term obscene.

Malcolm Boyd
Episcopal priest and gay activist

To focus on the private sex lives of lesbians and gays indicates several things about our society: First, focusing on sex distracts from real problems of poverty, war, etc. Second, preoccupation with our sex lives is a convenient means to ignore other aspects of our personal lives such as jobs and children. Third, it says a whole lot about the pleasures society derives from talking about the pleasures of sex everyone is supposed to deny.

It's sometimes difficult to put it all in perspective. However, while others focus on sex, we are busy integrating all aspects of our being . . . celebrating our sexuality and going on with our daily lives.

No one is free until everyone is free.

Phrase sung at the
1993 March on Washington

Our oppression is linked to oppression of other minorities. Each step our community takes for freedom is also a reminder of the prejudice other people face.

Each personal step we take as individuals to demand basic rights is a step toward freedom for all of us. Our individual acts contribute to a broader call for social justice.

Every cry for justice is a step in our own healing. We all heal by telling the world we will no longer be invisible by remaining silent.

Eden is that old-fashioned house
We dwell in every day.

Emily Dickinson
poet

Within ourselves is the Eden for which we search. Although we may look for acceptance and approval from others to help "make us happy," in essence our happiness and contentment come from our own self-approval.

The basis of our happiness must not rest on others' approval.

Affirmation comes from within. And when affirmation and pride are reclaimed, no one can take it away from us. It lies inside. It always has. Find it. Keep it.

Be Political, Not Polite.

Romanovsky & Phillips
singers/songwriters

One of the results of hearing a lot of shaming messages about homosexuality while growing up is a tendency to be overly nice, quiet and passive. This is exactly what some people wish lesbians and gays would do: "Don't rock the boat." "Keep it quiet." "Stay in the closet."

It's not that there's a problem with being polite or nice. There is a problem however, when our politeness results in passivity.

Think back to grade school. The kids who were overly nice oftentimes got pushed around.

Don't get pushed around. Be assertive when you need to!

Near fatal are chains that hold the mind captive; captive is the spirit that lacks freedom.

Jacquelyn Stapleton
writer

Prejudice and discrimination are the chains that attempt to keep lesbians and gays captive. However, these chains need not be fatal. How do we break the chains? Each time we validate ourselves as lesbians and gays we break a link in the chain. Every time we come out another link breaks.

Remember, once we reclaim our pride, no one can take it away from us. Prejudice and discrimination may continue, but our pride will free our spirits until the prejudice ends.

Everyone wants to be a dyke now; everyone craves our freedom, guts, and knowing looks.

Susie Bright
author

Being lesbian and gay is considered "fashionable" to some people. The attraction is not to those in the closet. Rather, the attraction is based on the courage of individuals who have reclaimed their pride and freely express themselves for who they are.

Freedom comes with courage. You have the courage. Are you using it?

[on being HIV+]: *There's a lot I want to do. Somehow I feel like the clock's ticking and I feel I don't want to die without someone to love. A greater injustice would be if I died without having loved myself.*

Jonathan Brown

Sometimes we live our lives without asking ourselves if we really love ourselves. We may act as if we probably do or perhaps, we don't ask the question because underneath we have not let go of all the shaming messages we grew up with about homosexuality.

To heal from heterosexism and to fully love ourselves we cannot take the chance to simply hope that age will bring self-love. To love ourselves, we must know ourselves.

Take time to slow down. Take time alone, to come to know yourself and to love yourself.

Today, after years of struggling with the shame of being different—a shame I think all gay people grow up with—I've learned that my difference is often my strength.

Dorothy Atcheson
writer

Taking the pain of the prejudice we have suffered and transforming it into a powerful life force that provides strength and courage, we move from victim to survivor. And then, we not only survive, but build on this foundation and thrive as lesbian and gay individuals.

Our challenge is to move forward, in spite of the prejudices we face. If we want to free our spirits, it is the only choice.

The books that the world calls immoral books are books that show the world its own shame.

Oscar Wilde
writer

Books banned or altered because of their homosexual or homo-erotic content are clear examples of society's irrational fear and shame about homosexuality.

Morality gets twisted into the likes and dislikes of the majority. Is it moral to silence a minority that is finally recognized by the educated as healthy, normal and posing no threat to society? Attempts to silence and control are the unrecognized but real immorality.

Breaking the silence surrounding the prejudices we face as lesbians and gays not only helps each of us in our individual healing process, but also expresses the immorality of others.

Discrimination hinders coming out.
Coming out hinders discrimination.

Unknown

We live in a world of contradictions. The push and pull of coming out is a very real struggle for lesbians and gays.

A myriad of factors influence our thoughts about coming out—family, job, children, safety and more. It's a continual juggling act of balancing out what will be gained from what might be lost. There can be a tendency to maximize the perceived losses by failing to differentiate between short- and long-term effects. Simultaneously, we minimize the emotional costs to ourselves of staying in the closet.

What is clear is that as more lesbians and gays come out, it will be plain to see "we are everywhere," making coming out less of a struggle and discrimination less likely.

The longest day must have it's close—the gloomiest night will wear on to a morning. An eternal inexorable lapse of moments is ever hurrying the day of evil to an eternal night, and the night of the just to an eternal day.

Harriet Beecher Stowe
writer

Nearly 150 years later these words ring true for the lesbian and gay community. Our oppression has been long and difficult. Throughout our oppression we have always found ways to survive and keep going. Our hope is our resiliency. Our belief that a caring world is possible and that with time society will acknowledge, redress and grieve with us their inhumanity to lesbians and gays, is also our resiliency.

Great change is happening now. Keep hope alive.

A lot of your life is wasted in trying to stay in the closet . . . I was worrying that if Stan saw a second toothbrush, he'd somehow figure out I was gay, which I was trying to avoid at all costs. And it suddenly hit me how ridiculous that was.

Fred Hersch
pianist/composer

Each time we hide, each time we keep silent about our homosexuality in the face of disparaging remarks about our very being, it's as if we take another blow when we are already on the floor.

As children we try to protect ourselves by saying the shaming messages "don't hurt." As we reach adolescence the blows to our self-esteem are commonplace but we have mastered our denial by believing no harm comes to us from the hurtful comments. Deep inside, however, our very souls are writhing in pain.

We have many chances to speak up and free our souls. Sometimes it feels safe, other times it doesn't. Grab the opportunities you can!

What is the answer? . . .
In that case, what is the question?

Gertrude Stein
writer

Who knows what life and death are all about? Without completely knowing the question or answer, I do know that happiness and contentment come with my attempts to be true to myself, living life to the best of my ability as I choose, and making my dreams happen.

Make your dreams happen now. Be the gay or lesbian individual you want to be so that life does not just pass you by.

You must do the thing you think you cannot do.

Eleanor Roosevelt

After years of socialization in which we heard erroneous and negative messages about homosexuality, it is not surprising to reach adulthood still feeling like others are in charge of our lives.

Healing from the negative effects of heterosexism involves taking charge of our lives. As we take the power back and take charge of our lives we realize that many of the things we thought we could not do are in fact quite simple to do. Walking down the street hand in hand is no longer impossible but instead liberating and exhilarating. Kissing our partner goodbye at the airport is no longer unthinkable, but natural, loving and an act of courage.

We must continue to tap the power that lies inside waiting to be freed. Anything becomes possible.

It's tremendously empowering when you're gay to realize that you've been doing it right, and it's the bigots who are stumbling about in a fog.

Howard Cruse
cartoonist

In the 1950s the prevailing mindset can be encapsulated in the words "the homosexual problem." Homosexuals were singled out, and carried the weight of prejudice on their shoulders.

In the 1970s some of the weight was taken off of our shoulders as people began to examine their homophobia.

Heterosexism is the theme of the 1990s. For those people who are still buying into prejudices about lesbians and gays: It's their problem, not ours!

We heal when we personally move from a place of viewing our homosexuality, as a problem to celebrating our homosexuality and recognizing that the people with the problems are the ones that won't let go of the myths and stereotypes about homosexuality.

[regarding people with AIDS]: *Each one of them is Jesus in a distressing disguise.*

Mother Teresa

The AIDS epidemic has brought out the best and worst in people. It is a litmus test of our humanity.

We can respond with cold indifference, hatred and bigotry, or with courage, compassion and love.

The lesbian and gay community has led the world in an outpouring of compassion and care. History will show our community as leaders in humanitarian efforts.

Take pride in your community.

We are a land of many colors, we are singing, singing for our lives.

Holly Near
singer/songwriter

Our world continues to grapple with the biases and prejudices we grew up with. The lesbian and gay community is at the forefront of dispelling these prejudices and recognizing the importance of celebrating diversity.

We are at the forefront because lesbians and gays cut across all segments of society. Sexual orientation knows no racial, ethnic, socio-economic, religious or cultural boundaries.

Our community is more diverse than any other. And we are joining hands. We must join hands. There is no other way.

Gay lives cannot be examined through straight spectacles.

Robert K. Martin
writer/critic

Other people have tried to explain lesbian and gay lives for decades without even asking us to share our voices. Implicit in this wayward approach is that heterosexuals must have superior insights about all things while homosexuals are incapable of accurately reflecting even on their own existence because they are inherently pathological.

It doesn't take a genius to recognize that we need to respect every individual's voice. This is why, my friend, you must raise your voice and share your story.

Don't let others speak for you. Don't let your voice go unheard. You owe it to yourself.

It is very easy for those of us who are truly open to the state of the world around us to give in to despair. But I know I must continue to fight, and that the battle is worthwhile. It did not begin with me nor will it end with me, but what I do is essential.

Audre Lorde
writer

Healing from the negative effects of heterosexism can periodically leave us feeling drained. Despair may set in as we look at the hatred and bigotry that still abound.

Anger and sadness are natural responses as we struggle for basic rights that others take for granted. Each bit of time and energy we utilize to personally heal from heterosexism is essential in this struggle. We are better able to continue the fight when we take care of ourselves.

As the fight continues we must remember it is a necessary fight, we will prevail and each contribution we make for change is essential.

Coming out proud, strong, and without apologies is the most effective way we as individuals and as a community can overcome the propagandist attacks we face.

Matteo Valenti
in letter in *Out* magazine

This is another reminder about the devastating effects of silence. Hiding the truth about who we are only contributes to further secrets and more lies. Hiding and silence fuel shame.

Each of us as lesbians and gays need to continue the process of being open and honest about our homosexuality. Keeping silent only perpetuates shame.

Find one more way to acknowledge and validate your homosexuality, and one more vestige of shame will be released today.

To love without role, without power plays, is revolution.

Rita Mae Brown
writer

Woman and woman, man and man—we change the harmful stereotypes that relationships need to be based on a dominant male and passive female.

Balanced relationships of man and man, woman and man or woman and woman are the only valid relationships. Can there be loving, caring and nurturing adult relationships when there is a power imbalance? Perhaps in certain situations, (e.g., when someone is ill). But to hold onto power-based gender-role stereotypes is reprehensible.

Our committed partnerships challenge harmful stereotypes. Take pride . . . we are doing more to change the world than we realize!

Gay is what God made me. Proud is what I choose to be.

Chris W.

Our gayness is a gift from God. It is part of our being that cannot be separated from other aspects of the self.

Being gay is not a choice. Repressing our gayness or embracing our gayness are the only choices. We can choose to be proud of who we are or continue to buy into the shaming myths and stereotypes about homosexuality we grew up with.

Choose pride. It is a healthy choice. It is affirming. It is what is needed to heal from the shaming messages society has promulgated.

*As a community we are taking our relation-
ships and families more seriously as we shift
from a movement based on individual rights
to one based on full equality as citizens in
all aspects of life.*

Paula Ettelbrick
National Center for Lesbian Rights

The lesbian and gay civil rights movement
continues to evolve. In the 1970s our motto
was "Gay is Okay." The 1980s ushered in "Gay
and Proud."

With, and only with, gay pride are we able
to demand full equality. As individuals we go
through a similar process from "I'm okay" to
"I'm proud" and eventually expecting and settling for no less than tolerance, respect and
equal civil rights.

Each of us must continue to take pride in
being lesbian and gay. Without this, we cannot
expect heterosexuals to fully accept and
respect us.

Our time has come America, our time has come!

Virginia Apuzzo
former executive director
National Lesbian and Gay Task Force (NLGTF)

The time for lesbian and gay civil rights is now. America can no longer deny that reality. Cities, towns, corporations and universities have already enacted policies and legislation to protect lesbians and gays. Federal lesbian and gay civil rights legislation is inevitable.

As individuals we may face frustration assessing the advances, setbacks and more advances. However, it is also a time to savor the tremendous amount of personal pride we can take for being involved in this historic fight for basic human rights.

Get involved! Take pride!

Queer by the grace of God

1990s bumper sticker

Do you view your homosexuality as a gift or a hindrance? As children we are usually taught to see it as a hindrance, on occasion as something "Okay" but rarely as a gift. Yet, it is a gift. We may not initially see it as a gift because we took for granted the message that homosexuality was a hindrance.

Healing involves re-examining these harmful stereotypes, then letting go of the myths so that each of us can make the personal transformation from homosexuality as a hindrance to homosexuality as a gift.

Nothing is lonelier in the whole world than a gay child. And I think all of us have that. . . . I have a lot of pride, and when people don't take me seriously, I get angry.

Edmund White
author

We grow up emotionally isolated because our families do not understand homosexuality, and then our access to the lesbian and gay community is limited.

As we grow older we have many more options, and much more access for support and validation. However, others will not take us seriously if we are isolated because our pride cannot develop in isolation.

Take advantage of your options and seek support. Reclaim your pride. Others will take note because our pride does not go unnoticed.

America is not a blanket woven from one thread, one color, one cloth. We must build a quilt together . . . Blacks and Hispanics, when we fight for civil rights, we are right—but our patch isn't big enough. Gays and lesbians, when you fight against discrimination . . . you are right—but your patch isn't big enough . . . But when we bring the patches together we make a quilt . . . Then we, the people, always win.

Jesse Jackson

People who have been victimized sometimes unleash their anger and frustration by victimizing others. We must continue to fight for the respect and dignity *all* individuals deserve.

It is not enough to be content with making progress toward eliminating heterosexism. We must continue to show how all forms of discrimination and prejudice are harmful. We ask for respect for all people.

[Regarding Gertrude Stein and Alice B. Toklas]: *And they were so emphatically and uncompromisingly themselves, that the world could do nothing less than accept them as they were.*

Diana Souhami
writer

As our partnerships grow, so do our love and commitment. The love of a nurturing and enduring relationship creates a bond that provides resiliency to a hostile world. The love we hold for each other provides a haven of safety. In this haven we have more freedom to be who we are unencumbered.

Over the years this protective, loving haven provides strength so that what others think no longer matters. We know our love is fulfilling. As that truth grows stronger within us nothing can shake the bonds we have established.

I am proud to be a gay man because it has taught me to be true to my instincts for love and affection in the face of discrimination, threats of imprisonment and danger of death.

John G.

We need to take pride each time we are true to ourselves, each time we are open about our sexual orientation. These are acts of courage. They are daily acts of rebellion.

We must continue to give ourselves credit for the steps we take on a daily basis to empower ourselves, and to heal from the abusiveness of living in a heterosexist society.

Take pride in your courage and the courage of your community. It is remarkable, beautiful and inspiring!

....

Home is the definition of God.

Emily Dickinson
poet

Home is the inner peace we create for ourselves. We carry it no matter where we travel. And without this sense of inner peace, no matter where we travel, we will never feel "at home."

We can move miles from family and old friends to hide our homosexuality, but distance alone cannot create inner peace. It involves being honest with ourselves and others . . . no matter where we live. Then we can truly "be at home."

By staying closeted we make ourselves invisible; by coming out we shatter the popular illusion that the whole world is heterosexual.

Romanovsky & Phillips
singers/songwriters

Legislators often say "But there aren't any gays in my district." They don't see us; they don't think we exist. They don't receive our calls and letters and they think the only calls are from heterosexuals.

There are lots of ways to be visible. Write a letter . . . and say you're gay. Your voice is important. Let someone know you're out there. It's the first step in letting them know you matter.

I'll be here tomorrow and tomorrow and tomorrow.

sung by Lorna Luft
at the 1993 March on Washington

Gays and lesbians are not going away. For those who choose to deny we exist today, they must still face us tomorrow. For those who hope we'll retreat to the silence of the closet today, they will find more lesbians and gays out of the closet tomorrow, visible and proud.

Where do you stand today? Where do you want to be tomorrow? How long will it take you to make your tomorrow come true? What are you waiting for?

There is only one real deprivation . . . and that is not to be able to give one's gifts to those one loves most.

May Sarton
poet

It is difficult to share our gifts with our families and friends when we are in the closet. Think of the volunteer work done for AIDS organizations or gay and lesbian teen groups that goes unnoticed. Or that lesbian or gay chorus you're involved with but Mom and Dad don't know about.

Don't deprive yourself of the recognition you deserve for your gifts, your skills and the activities you are involved with. Share your gifts by finding one more way to come out.

I leave you the will to fight, the desire to live, the right to anger, to love, to joy, to transform silence into language and action. I leave you a litany for survival.

Audre Lorde
writer

Surviving and thriving: The lesbian and gay community moves from silence to action.

On an individual level, our personal growth also depends on transforming silence into action. Silence results in stagnation. We cannot maximize our potential by staying in the closet. Move from silence into action. Come out of the closet into personal growth and maturity.

[Regarding the 1993 March on Washington]: *The million of us converging on Washington signals a force of justice that will not—and cannot—be stopped.*

John D'Emilio
gay historian

When individuals and communities recognize the victimization they have endured and then begin to take pride in themselves, it becomes clear that once pride is secured demands for justice will not cease.

To have pride is to expect justice. Only with pride are we able to fight for justice.

Our individual acts of reclaiming pride, whether we recognize it or not, are continual calls for justice.

(At the 1993 March on Washington): *Our strength is our diversity.*

Antonio Pagan
New York city council member

We were taught to place a superior value on all things white, male and heterosexual, to name a few. Why has society turned its back on the few voices celebrating diversity? The insecurity of those holding power often silences those who challenge the status quo, for it may mean giving up some of their power and learning to share power.

Power cannot be maintained endlessly by limiting access to others. We are beginning to recognize that power needs to be shared. It is not only that our strength is our diversity, but our hope lies in celebrating our diversity.

The numbers in Washington were not as important as the faces, the sheer humanity of one person after another stepping forward, saying, "Look at me. I am a cop, a mother, a Catholic, a Republican, a soldier, an American." So the ice melts. The hate abates. The numbers, finally, all come down to one.

Anna Quindlen

We frequently underestimate the impact of singular, personal acts of coming out. When our parents and co-workers saw news coverage of the 1993 March on Washington, a common response was surprise at the numbers. It remained impersonal and lacked meaning until thousands of us went back home and came out. We put faces on the marchers. We made it personal and therefore understandable.

Don't underestimate the power of one . . . *your* power.

It's the most unhappy people who most fear change.

Mignon McLaughlin

To live is to change. To fear change is to fear life itself. Living in continual fear can only result in stagnation and discontent.

We are taught to fear our homosexuality. We release this fear as we dispel the myths and stereotypes we were taught. These shaming messages may be so ingrained that we do not realize we have internalized them.

Go back and re-examine these myths. Each time you dispel a myth you move forward in celebrating yourself.

We must overcome our fears to fully live.

The days are gone when everything is happening in New York or San Francisco.

Didier Heiremana
Human Rights Campaign Fund

Lesbian and gay visibility is increasing across the country. Though major metropolitan areas continue to be the hub of lesbian and gay activities, smaller cities, towns and rural areas offer a growing number of social and support outlets. There are now gay and lesbian political caucuses across the country ... athletic teams, musical organizations, psychologist associations, religious groups, 12-step meetings and much more.

We no longer have to live in isolation. Reach out and join in. Building community is building family ... a family of pride.

I never needed saving from anything except the cruel and ignorant piety of people like Anita Bryant.

Armistead Maupin
author

How ironic! The people we most need saving from are the same people who claim to be trying to save us! The arrogance and ignorance of these people is revolting. Their message is shaming. They attempt to hide the abusiveness of their words and actions by claiming it is in the name of Christian salvation.

Christianity is not based on hatred and bigotry. Thankfully, a growing number of friends recognize the hatred veiled in this religious fanaticism.

Surround yourself with those people who accept and value you for who you are.

Not "special" rights but equal rights.

banner at the
1993 March on Washington

In attempts to stall our fight for equal rights, some individuals purport that we are asking for special rights.

Protection from losing our jobs simply because we are gay is not a "special" right. It's a basic human right.

Protection from being harassed in our homes or kicked out of our homes is not a special right. Our demands for equal rights are fair and just.

Each of us must continue to speak up and demand equal rights, simply because we deserve them.

I Don't Mind Straight People
As Long As They Act Gay In Public

T-shirt slogan

Sometimes turning the tables is the only way heterosexuals "get it." The irony of such humor can be used to help educate. Sometimes humor is the most effective way of communicating. And in this case, we get to have some fun while pointing out a powerful message.

Let yourself laugh! Healing involves some fun, too.

Homosexual affection can be as selfless as heterosexual affection, and therefore we cannot see that it is in some way morally wrong. An act which expresses true affection between two individuals and gives pleasure to them both does not seem to us to be sinful simply because it is homosexual.

Anonymous

The voice of reason is often concealed in the clamor of a sometimes crazy world. Though it may be concealed, do not forget that the voice of reason does exist.

Sweep aside the noise. When the noise settles, the simple truths will be clear.

It's not mental illness but homophobia . . . that is pushing a lot of gay teens to kill themselves.

Kenny Dayton
from letter in *Advocate* magazine

Critics of lesbians and gays predict homosexuality will somehow destroy civilization. It will not, but hatred and bigotry will. Spreading hatred results in individuals who either learn to hate themselves or learn to hate those who are different from themselves.

Upon releasing the hate-filled messages we grew up with, we learn to love both ourselves and others. Our community is filled with loving, caring people striving to make a better world free of hatred and bigotry. Each time we release a piece of the hate that others have tried to force on us, we provide hope for a better future because it provides an opportunity to bestow understanding and compassion where once there was hate. A heart that has released hate cannot pass on hate.

I am proud to be a gay man because gay culture has taught me to appreciate beauty and proportion, wit and creativity.

John G.

Gay people have expressed their sense of beauty throughout all times and ages. Attempts to hide the sexuality of great artists such as Michelangelo and others have failed.

Perhaps gay people do have a special proclivity to appreciate beauty and proportion. Indeed, some societies have elevated homosexual members to a special status because of their insights, abilities and creativity.

In recent years we have certainly shown our ability to laugh in spite of adversity.

Kate Clinton, Tom Amiano and others have taught us to take time to laugh. And we should take time to reflect on what special people we are.

She seemed sorrowful, a thousand-year-old woman. I recognized in her the young woman I had been until not so long ago. I took her hand which was resting on the beige comforter. The two of us had come from such different experiences, but in some way we were the same.

Sara Levi Calderon
author

Lesbians and gays, all backgrounds and all ages have something to share with each other and much to learn from each other.

The prejudices we have faced have kept us from reaching out towards each other. It's time for each of us to take note and move beyond differences of age, race or any other ways that we are somehow "different" from others.

Passion, knowledge, love and wisdom can be found in the most unexpected places if you keep your heart and mind open.

You can be strong in the bad times. . . .
Believe in yourself.

N. Swanston and T. Cox
songwriters

Within each of us is an inner strength that gets buried away as a result of years of discrimination and prejudice. We catch glimpses of it. And, we know it is still there, but struggle with accessing it.

As we struggle in difficult times, as we struggle with self-acceptance, we need to continue to trust our intuition. Each time we trust our intuition that being gay is healthy and normal we help solidify a positive image of ourselves as lesbian or gay. We relearn to believe in ourselves and affirm that inner strength that will not die.

Believe in yourself!

....

If you want to know who the oppressed minorities in America are, you simply look at who gets their own shelf in the bookstore. A black shelf, a woman's shelf, and a gay shelf.

Armistead Maupin
author

Before bigotry and oppression were exposed there were no gay bookstores or "gay shelves" in mainstream bookstores. As the prejudices are revealed, gays and lesbians raise their voices and their pens! Our critics will say, "Why do we need a gay section? There's not a straight section." Remember, heterosexual voices are validated every second of every day. Gay and lesbian voices have been silenced for generations.

Until our voices are heard universally, we will need our own forum as a message that silence is not acceptable.

Coming out separates the wheat from the chaff. . . . You learn who your friends really are.

Fred Hersch
from letter in *Advocate* magazine

We do not need society's acceptance to personally affirm our homosexuality. Society's acceptance is wanted and with time it will come, but we cannot wait for others to validate us before we affirm ourselves. As we have learned from gay and lesbian voices from the past, it is possible to affirm ourselves despite formidable oppression. It is possible because in our hearts and in the depths of our souls we intuitively know our homosexuality is a gift, just as our hands, minds and voices are unique gifts.

Self-acceptance grows from within. Nurture your gifts, including your homosexuality. Your true friends will be there to stand by you.

Remember the past, influence your future.

1984 Gay/Lesbian
Pride Celebration slogan

Remember the silence of the past and the struggles of lesbians and gays forced into the closet. Rediscover the vibrant history of previous generations and be humble in the face of the true leaders of the lesbian and gay community: our courageous sisters and brothers who risked all and still spoke out for acceptance of homosexuality. Their courage has bolstered countless lesbians and gays to speak out against prejudice and discrimination today.

Remembering the past inspires us to influence the future. We must take the opportunity to do so now, in a climate that is much more conducive to acceptance and change.

Take one small step today to make this a better world for yourself and other lesbians and gays.

The greatest tool the oppressor has is the mind of the oppressed.

G. Carter Woodson
historian

Heterosexism and homophobia leave lesbians and gays thinking like victims: giving up easy and giving up hope. We start acting like victims and don't realize it. We don't finish that college degree or pursue that work promotion because on some innermost level we have internalized the message that "gays are not successful." We learn to act out a self-fulfilling prophecy of "I'm not okay."

The effects of heterosexism are far more pervasive than meets the eye. Take time to examine every behavior and thought to insure that you continue to release the power of the shaming messages we grew up with.

We had one young man who was a throw-away from Boston. He thought that he could share his being gay with them [his parents]. They threw him out of the house. He never went home. But he had us.

Joyce Hunter
co-founder
Harvey Milk High School
for Lesbian and Gay Teens

Finally, lesbians and gays are beginning to take the responsibility to care for lesbian and gay youth. Our hesitancy in meeting this challenge stems in part from our very own internalization of the child-molesting myth.

Lesbians and gays are already fine parents. Lesbians and gays are already respected child-care workers and teachers.

Debunk the myth and show what we already know to be true. By doing so, we will also open a door of support for lesbian and gay youth.

They're trying to take away my pride . . .
They're trying to hurt me inside . . .
I ain't been knocked down yet . . .
I was born to fight.

Tracy Chapman
singer/songwriter

Where is your fighting spirit? Your will to
survive? Has it been buried after the years of
discrimination and covered with the resulting
pain?

The pain is released each time you share
your story, each time you talk about what it
was like growing up lesbian or gay. As you
release the pain, you will rediscover the will to
live. You will rediscover your pride, and that's
what makes life worth living.

Intimacy is the touching of hearts.

Sally Fisher
educator/writer
AIDS Mastery Workshop

To say that heterosexual love is superior to homosexual love misses the bigger picture. More important is the capacity to be intimate and share love.

Love is tenderness, caring and passion that comes from the soul. To say that heartfelt and nurturing homosexual love is invalid simply because we are homosexual is a sign of ignorance and a fear of love itself. What's the point of trying to categorize love? We must remember that love exists because it is a part of being human.

Don't deny yourself the capacity to love because you're gay. Simply stated, it cannot be denied—because love is love.

If we do not allow numbers to define us but demand our place in the sun, loudly and queerly showing and telling, then our numbers will also increase.

Larry Gross
professor
University of Pennsylvania

The number of lesbians and gays is a moot point. More important is the ability of lesbians and gays to be ourselves and live our lives without fear of recrimination because of our sexuality. Lack of societal support keeps many gays from realizing this freedom. And this is exactly what people who harbor prejudices against us hope will happen as a result of their efforts to discourage anything "pro gay."

Be yourself. Be open and proud. Recognize the power of one.

....

We have all known the long loneliness and we have learned that the only solution is love and that love comes with community.

Dorothy Day

Growing up isolated as lesbians and gays we wonder how we can ever be ourselves and how we can ever realize our dreams.

Our lifeline is finding other lesbians and gays who accept and love us for who we are. We need validation from our own community when we are not getting it in other places.

Make connections with *your* community. The lesbian and gay community is diverse, so search until you find your place. Transform community to family.

I found Queequeg's arm thrown over me in the most loving and affectionate manner. . . . Thus, then in our heart's honeymoon, lay I and Queequeg a cozy, loving pair . . . He pressed his forehead against mine, clasped me around the waist, and said henceforth we were married.

Herman Melville
writer

References to homosexual love are found in many of the great literary classics. How often were these references deleted, altered or simply not discussed? And what is the result?

Gays and non-gays grow up reading only about heterosexual love. Prejudices are fostered by the message, "There's only one way to love," which is simply not true. As we re-expose these classics, we give the world the opportunity to see our love has always existed, and always will.

Beneath the duality of sex there is a oneness. Every male is potentially a female and every female potentially a male. If a man wants to understand a woman, he must discover the woman in himself, and if a woman would understand a man, she must dig in her own consciousness to discover her own masculine traits.

Magnus Hirschfeld
sexologist and early homosexual rights activist

Every heterosexual is potentially a homosexual, and every homosexual is potentially a heterosexual. If a heterosexual wants to understand a homosexual, the individual must discover the homosexual within. And if a homosexual would understand a heterosexual, the individual must dig in his own consciousness to discover heterosexual traits.

Homosexuality and heterosexuality are not the discrete categories we once believed. What do you think?

When the dust settles and the pages of history are written, it will not be the angry defenders of intolerance who have made the difference. That reward will go to those who have dared to step outside the safety of their privacy in order to expose and rout the prevailing prejudices.

John Shelby Spong
Episcopal bishop

Every time we speak out against injustice, write letters to the editor, call our legislators or come out to bosses, we change history.

At the time, we may ask ourselves "What difference does it make anyway?" It makes a big difference. The cumulative effect of each one of our actions is at the core of society's education about lesbians and gays.

You don't need to be a Harvey Milk or Virginia Apuzzo to change history. One action on your part, however small, starts a ripple that helps build the wave of change.

It's not the pot that grows the flower.
It's not the clock that slows the hour.
The definition's plain for anyone to see.
Love is all it takes to make a family.

> Romanovsky & Phillips
> singers/songwriters

All this fuss about who is family and who is not. We already know a minority of families constitute the picture of a "traditional" family with Mom, Dad and 2.2 kids. Yet, some people still try to force this definition as the only definition of family.

As lesbians and gays we know better. We have already established all sorts of families. And our families are based on love. We do not have the hypocrisy of spewing hatred toward loving families!

We will continue to form families because love cannot be stopped and we have a lot of love to give.

Love Makes A Family

> gay and lesbian parents banner
> at the 1993 March on Washington

The 1990s has brought an increase in discussions on redefining family. In some ways we do need to redefine families and in other ways we do not.

The structure of families has changed over the decades, but the function of families has remained the same. We see more single parent families, and lesbian and gay parents are becoming more visible as increasing numbers of lesbian and gay couples are adopting children. In this sense, we are redefining families because we recognize the many existing family forms. However, the functions remain the same: to love, to nurture and to support.

Lesbians and gays have and continue to create loving, caring families. Love and nurturing are more important than one particular family form because without love a family cannot exist.

[At the 1993 March on Washington]: *We all believe in America that has not been yet. And, in the words of Langston Hughes, "I too sing America, the America that has never been yet, but yet must be."*

Ken Reeves
mayor of Cambridge, Massachusetts

The "land of the free" will not be free until all of its citizens are free. Lesbians and gays are one of the last minorities to demand basic civil rights.

Freedom is not about one group maintaining their power and control over others so that they can keep their "freedom." Freedom will elude us until we learn to co-exist.

We must all learn to accept and respect those different from ourselves. It is only in respecting differences that we understand the similarities that bring all people together.

Society tells us that if we remain silent, if we keep our place, we can live. But if we cross the line and we are too visible, we might just die. . . . I was quoted in the Juneau newspaper . . . as a lesbian . . . it was the scariest line to cross, but I'm glad I did it because now there is no turning back.

Sara Boesser
gay rights activist

Silence and invisibility provide only a false sense of protection. The insecurity of the closet reminds us that silence does not fully protect us.

Visibility provides protection because with it comes power: the power of self-confidence and pride. As more lesbians and gays come out, the power of our community multiplies exponentially.

Protect yourself best by choosing pride.

Many thousands of gay people who had never participated in gay rights efforts were motivated to join the fight against AIDS.

Eric Marcus
author

Our motivation to fight AIDS is based on our righteous anger and the deep love we have for our sisters and brothers. Our community has led the fight against AIDS. We are the primary caregivers. We fight to end discrimination. We demand a more aggressive search for treatments and a cure.

We cannot wait for others to do what we wish for, but must instead continue our outpouring of love and compassion. In doing so, the world takes note of the compassionate, caring and loving nature of the lesbian and gay community.

Get involved. Take pride in our community. We are truly leaders.

If you went into a class of thirty, there had to be a couple of gay people in that class. My being there would let them know that there were other gay people, that they weren't alone, and they were okay. You see, growing up, I didn't know what it meant to be gay . . . I wanted to change that.

Joyce Hunter
co-founder
Harvey Milk High School
for Lesbian and Gay Teens

The goal of education is to open young minds. Yet, frequently we limit its discourse. It is not surprising then, that children don't know a thing about homosexuality.

Growing up with the lack of information about homosexuality propels many of us to provide the education we did not receive. We are the true educators with our goals of openness and understanding, not rigidity and intolerance.

I know I can't tell you what it is to be gay. But I can tell you what it's not. It's not hiding behind words, Mama. Like family and decency and Christianity. It's not fearing your body, or the pleasures that God made for it. It's not judging your neighbor, except when he's cross or unkind.

Armistead Maupin
author

As part of our process of embracing and celebrating being gay, we are forced to re-examine many notions about family, sexuality, religion and much more. And how much richer we are from the personal introspection this entails!

Many non-gays go through life placidly accepting cultural norms without batting an eye. Personal growth and development only come with deep self-examination.

Our gayness propels us to know ourselves better—another reason to be thankful for being gay!

Being visible can make us free . . . and give us a power we have never known.

Katherine V. Forrest
writer

Society is still slow to acknowledge its abusive treatment of lesbians and gays. What we have to our advantage that previous generations of lesbians and gays did not have is a much more visible and vocal lesbian and gay community. Our community continues to shout, "We will no longer accept or tolerate your hateful and abusive treatment of us. We demand respect and won't stop until we get it!" Past generations could only dream of the support and power we have today.

Too many lesbians and gays today still sit back and don't make our voices heard. This is synonymous with sitting back passively like a victim who does not heal.

Are you doing your part by shouting loudly? Your voice deserves and needs to be heard. Find a way to do your part.

Life was meant to be lived, and curiosity must be kept alive. One must never, for whatever reason, turn his back on life.

Eleanor Roosevelt

We live in a world that encourages us to turn our back on our homosexuality. We do not fully live when we deny an essential part of who we are.

Reclaiming our homosexuality is saying "yes" to life. Whether you do an "about face" or gradual turn, take your next step in living the life you want to have. One step is fine for today.

I don't think there is a heterosexual marriage in this country that would exist with the absence of support that we give to gay couples . . . I think we ought to take off our hats to them and cheer. I think they've got something to teach the rest of us about a holy relationship.

John Shelby Spong
Episcopal bishop

We form healthy, viable, loving relationships despite the tremendous prejudice we face. Our lasting relationships are a testimony of our love and commitment. Sometimes we do not take notice within our own community of these lasting relationships. We learn not to see them because we have been taught they don't exist. They do exist!

Just as we need more enlightened indviduals like Bishop Spong to recognize our relationships, we must take time to stop participating in the myths that our relationships don't last by seeing and supporting gay relationships.

If one homosexual in Altoona will never have to be invisible again, then I will have done my job.

Harvey Milk
former San Francisco city supervisor

Heterosexism and homophobia leave lesbians and gays vulnerable. Vulnerable because lesbians and gays are kept invisible so that initially we believe we are alone and we lose hope of the possibility of a positive future. When we believe we are alone and have lost hope, the pressure to conform to heterosexuality only increases.

When lesbians and gays are invisible, heterosexuality appears to be the only choice. Our visibility provides support and community. Our visibility provides hope for those who are pressured to remain locked in the closet. We no longer need to feel alone. Come out. Spread hope.

If you removed all of the homosexuals and homosexual influence from what is generally regarded as American culture, you would be pretty much left with Let's Make a Deal.

Fran Lebowitz

Perhaps as outsiders we have been forced to look at how banal American life can be. Or perhaps gay people have a proclivity to the creative and discerning. Is it possible that this creativity develops partly as a result of society's attempt to silence us? Then again, in some societies homosexuals have been revered as special and gifted.

For whatever reason, lesbians and gays are often on the cutting edge of what shapes culture. We set the pace in music, architecture, fashion, literature and more only to find mainstream America eager to catch up years later.

We create culture while so often others simply follow.

If through Gay Games and the Procession of the Arts we can characterize our own culture as one of tolerance and understanding, then we have a vehicle through which we can begin to teach others.

Tom Waddell
Olympic athlete and
founder of the Gay Games

Openly celebrating our talents, skills and accomplishments teaches the world about who we are. When we respect and honor ourselves we send a message to the world that we take pride in who we are. Simultaneously, we extend an invitation to others to come and celebrate with us. As others join our celebrations the human heart is enriched. As we join in celebration of both our differentness and sameness we foster tolerance, acceptance and love—love that knows no bounds.

Let's celebrate who we are. Slowly the world will join us in our celebration.

You withhold the parts of yourself that you think will be unacceptable. Your survival mechanisms replace your availability and vulnerability. You give your power away to be liked, loved and accepted.

Sally Fisher
educator/writer
AIDS Mastery Workshop

Being true to oneself is necessary to heal from heterosexism. Each time we hide our sexuality we are wounded again, destroying our self-esteem. Because we have been so shamed by society we begin to look to others for validation. We become what they want and what is acceptable to them. They love us not for who we are, but for who they want us to be.

Living a lie has a price that is too high: loss of our self-esteem. We may lose people in our lives once we stop hiding, but we will have our self-respect and will find other people who accept us for who we are.

If others do not accept me because I am gay, it is now their problem, not mine.

What a minority group wants is not the right to have geniuses among them but the right to have fools and scoundrels without being condemned as a group.

Agnes Elizabeth Benedict

It's common for oppressed individuals who have been told they are "screwed up" to play out a "screwed up" life, or to do just the opposite (i.e., be the best or be perfect). Sometimes this drive for perfectionism is based on a deep rooted sense of inferiority. Do you sometimes think "If I'm perfect, they can't help but accept me, even if I'm gay?"

It's okay to have goals and to take pride in your accomplishments. But when your accomplishments become the sole basis of your self-esteem, you have got a problem.

You deserve to be respected for who you are, not just for what you do. Are you basing your self-esteem on what you do rather than who you are?

If our American way of life fails the child, it fails us all.

Pearl Buck
writer

American life does not safeguard lesbian and gay children. Most Americans still believe that all children are born heterosexual. This leads to a lack of respect for lesbian and gay children and teens, and their needs go unmet.

Americans easily profess the importance of taking care of our children, yet lesbian and gay children remain unrecognized and therefore ignored.

The struggle to provide school curriculum that shows the diversity of Americans, including its lesbian and gay members, is a reminder of how far we have to go to teach respect and tolerance for those different than ourselves.

We have the opportunity and the obligation to be out so that lesbian and gay children do not grow up in fear and isolation as many of us did. Remember your pain. Help a child today.

I'm very militant, you know, in a quiet way.

Christopher Isherwood
writer

The lesbian and gay civil rights movement is not built on mass demonstration or the efforts of our leaders alone. Each one of us plays an active role in our daily lives. Our actions may not make the news and may seem unimportant, but going through our daily routine as openly lesbian and gay individuals is revolutionary.

When lesbian and gay couples attend their children's school conferences, barriers are broken. When we kiss our partner goodbye at the airport, our homosexuality cannot be dismissed. When we attend AA meetings and say "I'm Joe, gay, sober and proud," we foster change.

Each personal action, however small, is ultimately a political statement.

As we learn from each other
We start to glow.

N. Swanston and T. Cox
songwriters

Lesbians and gays who support each other and share their stories grow stronger and more proud. Remember the first time we found other lesbian and gay friends? The excitement, the relief, the joy! Finally coming into our own, with our own people, we discovered a whole new world outside of the closet.

Our newfound family fuels an inner flame —a flame of hope and renewal. Keep the flame burning by creating your own family—people who love and accept you for who you are.

There's no question about it: If everybody who's gay was visible, we would probably eliminate 70% of the oppression. Everybody already knows gay people. They just don't know that we're gay.

Jean O'Leary
former co-executive director
National Lesbian and Gay Task Force (NLGTF)

Lesbian and gay visibility hinders oppression. We do have a role in eliminating the oppression we suffer. We didn't cause, nor do we deserve the oppression, but our visibility certainly helps end discrimination.

As we come out to more people, remember how many times we feared an adverse reaction to our coming out only to find someone saying, "I already knew," "Oh, no big deal" or "I'm gay, too!" Coming out isn't always as difficult as we think.

Don't let your fear stop you from coming out.

Hate is not a family value.

1990s T-shirt slogan

To think that people filled with hate and fear had anything to tell us about family values! We have been courageous in establishing our own families, thereby challenging society to see the true meaning of family—to nurture, to care for, to support and to love those individuals one holds dear.

Each day we allow others to see the families we have created, we chip away at society's denial of our inherent capacity to form nurturing, caring and loving families. And, as the diversity of our families shows through, we will have taught society to look beyond the makeup of families and to focus on the loving and nurturing that truly defines families. We are family, too!

Heterosexism knocks you down
But pick yourself up off the ground . . .
When heterosexism strikes, strike back!

Romanovsky and Phillips
singers/songwriters

Heterosexism is one form of cultural victimization. Victimization leaves people feeling helpless, hopeless and acting like victims.

We are taught to believe that lesbians and gays are weak and we frequently reach adulthood feeling weak.

Do what you can do to say no to heterosexism. You have more strength than you may realize. It's just under the surface waiting to be tapped.

I think it pisses God off if you walk by the color purple in a field somewhere and don't notice it.

Alice Walker
writer

Red and blue are symbols of femininity and masculinity. Mixed together they become purple. Purple is the color of lesbian and gay pride.

Our society elevates masculinity and subordinates femininity. We celebrate both the masculine and feminine within each individual. One without the other loses the richness of purple.

How appropriate that the color purple symbolizes our expression of pride!

One does not die from pain unless one chooses to.

Wakako Yamauchi

Lesbians and gays are subjected to a great deal of pain in our society. We have choices about what we can do with that pain. When our pain immobilizes us we must try to reach out to someone who accepts and loves us.

Are there times, however, when you hang on to your pain for some sort of secondary "gain"? Is staying miserable sometimes about not wanting to move on, not wanting to take responsibility for your life?

We often have more options than we realize. Are you keeping yourself stuck or are you choosing healthy options for yourself?

[Upon coming out at age 67]:*The choice for me is not whether or not I am a gay man, but whether or not I am honest about who I am with myself and others. It is a choice to take down the wall of silence I have built around an important and vital part of my life; to end the separation and isolation I have imposed on myself all these years.*

Otis Charles
Episcopal bishop

Lesbian and gay people come out at all different ages. Increasingly so, we are coming out at every age, from the very young to the very old. There is not a "right" or "wrong" age to come out. However, the only tragedy is *never* coming out.

Break down the closet walls. It is *never* too late to come out. And it is never too late to take another step out.

MAY 13

[Regarding the need for mandatory lesbian/gay school curricula rather than "teacher discretion" in discussing lesbian/gay issues]: *It's never too early to teach prejudice prevention. Would you leave to teacher discretion the teaching of the importance of Martin Luther King?*

Shelly Weis
mother and Lesbian Avenger

Teacher discretion is a squeamish and unacceptable way of promoting tolerance. Tolerance is learned just as hatred is learned. Which do we want to teach?

Our efforts at including gay sensitive school curricula is not to "promote" homosexuality, but instead to teach tolerance instead of violence and hatred. Many teachers are coming out publicly and leading this fight. Speak up for these teachers, for our children's sake.

What wasn't possible a decade ago is slowly becoming a reality. Our children will thank us.

I want to make films that girls in malls will see, and when they leave, they'll say, "Being a lesbian looks great, I really want to be one!"

Maria Maggenti
film student
New York University

Lesbians and gays have always been on the cutting edge. Initially, the cutting edge can bring disdain. But eventually, it is viewed as fashionable, avante garde, cool! This becomes the next step in greater tolerance and acceptance of homosexuality.

Today lesbian and gay images are more available to teenagers. There is a growing number of teens who are considered cool because they are gay or hang with a gay crowd.

As more youth emulate these cutting-edge teens, we will have teens who challenge their parents ill-conceived notions about homosexuality. Who would have thought that it couldn't be finer than being lesbian or gay?

But merely of two simple men I saw today on the pier in the midst of the crowd, parting the parting of dear friends, the one to remain hung on the other's neck and passionately kissed him. While the one to depart tightly pressed the one to remain in his arms.

Walt Whitman
poet

Look at the love we share and make no mistake, it is undeniably beautiful. The power behind our open displays of affection is not founded solely on the courage of these acts, but more so on the natural beauty of tender, loving moments shared together. Love is beautiful because of this tenderness, not because of the gender of the individuals.

Embrace, nurture and celebrate the love we have for each other. It is beautiful, simply and undeniably beautiful.

Heterosexual weddings are society's way of saying "congratulations for successfully being heterosexual."

Gerald Loewen
Ph.D. candidate in child psychology
University of Minnesota

Affirmation for heterosexual individuals is found in every aspect of our society and every minute of the day. Therefore, heterosexual affirmation is not needed, but affirmation of lesbians and gays is needed.

Remember that mixture of emotions at heterosexual weddings? Happiness for the couple, yet sadness and anger for the lack of recognition and support for our relationships.

Lesbians and gays must build in their own daily affirmations. If we don't affirm ourselves, who will? We do not have the luxury of waiting for heterosexual approval. Today I proclaim I am gay and proud.

We are your family, your co-workers, your friends . . . you love us already.

Sara Boesser
sign carried at the 1987
March on Washington

How can someone stop loving us merely because they find out we are lesbian or gay? Is it ignorance? Or is it fear? How unfortunate. And mostly it's unfortunate because it is their loss, not ours. Their loss because while our love continues theirs is constrained by rigid stereotypes. We may want their love, but we do not need their love in order to go on with our lives.

Do not take the weight of their loss and place it on your shoulders by insisting they must love you. We must not base our self-esteem on others' approval. Instead, love yourself, and surround yourself with those people who love and accept you for who you are. These people are our families.

Hiding leads nowhere except to more hiding.

Margaret A. Robinson

Remember those times we hid our homosexuality from someone only to find that it made it more difficult when we eventually came out to them? Each time we hide the pattern becomes more entrenched making it more difficult to come out. Think, instead, of how unhindered you have felt when you did choose to be open about your homosexuality.

Openness leads to more openness: No more hiding. No more secrets. Free to do as you please. Free to be who you are.

MAY 19

Heroes take journeys, confront dragons and discover the treasure of their true selves.

Carol Pearson

Coming out is a journey. It is a healing process—a process of healing from cultural victimization, from facing one's homosexuality to accepting and taking pride in all that there is about being lesbian and gay.

It is a heroic act each time a lesbian or gay individual faces society's contempt and still chooses to come out. Take pride. You are a hero.

Danny came to understand the rules better: You had to make it by the police, pass as straight to your boss, and not let anybody know . . . psychologists said that homosexuals liked to flirt with danger—more evidence that they were sick. No one ever said homosexuals flirted with danger because heterosexuals had made the world a very dangerous place for them.

Randy Shilts
journalist/author

Most nongay people don't realize they have created an oppressive social climate for lesbians and gays. Being unaware of their own heterosexism, they teach lesbians and gays that "homosexuality is inherently problematic," rather than recognizing how their narrow perspective of the world is destructive. This socialization causes many lesbians and gays to grow up viewing their homosexuality, rather than others' heterosexism, as the problem.

Put the weight and blame where it belongs.

When I think of the family and friends whose respect I have earned by being honest, then I am grateful to be gay because I'm grateful to be myself and to be loved for it.

Arnie Kantrowitz
writer

The pride we feel in being true to ourselves and in being honest with family and friends about our homosexuality radiates from our being. Though we cannot predict whether others will respect us for being out, it is true that self-respect is founded on our ability to be honest with ourselves. And, with bigotry aside, others do respect us for being true to ourselves.

The challenges we face in accepting ourselves propels us to a deeper self-awareness which fosters greater self-love.

I am proud to be a gay man because my gay-ness has impelled me to a deeper spiritual life.

John G.

Numerous traditional religious institutions have tried to convince lesbians and gays that it is not possible for us to embrace spirituality because of our sexual orientation. On the contrary, our sexual orientation and the religious abuse we have suffered have propelled us to examine our spirituality in much more depth than many heterosexuals can ever hope to do.

Ours is not a spirituality that is measured by the number of times we attend a church service. Instead, it is a deep personal examination about the meaning of life, our role in life, how our gayness can be celebrated and how our gifts can be shared rather than stifled.

Being gay does not preclude spirituality. Openly embracing one's gayness is a form of spirituality.

*In the Forties the bomb dropped. In the
Forties the entire planet was threatened bio-
logically . . . why are we being intimidated
by a bunch of jerks who don't know anything about life? Who were they to tell us
what to feel and how we're supposed to
behave?*

Allen Ginsberg
poet

To try to argue that homosexuality is
immoral when we live in a society that continues to commit immoral offenses is absurd. It
certainly takes the focus off the harm done in
other areas.

The time and energy America spends in victimizing lesbians and gays could certainly be
better spent.

Remember, because one holds power does
not mean one holds wisdom or knowledge.

Gay people don't need any more screen martyrs.

Howard Rosenman
film producer

Until recently the only depictions of gays on film and television were portrayals of people who were not emotionally stable. Despite solid research indicating that sexual orientation in and of itself does not determine mental health, the media continues to perpetuate the myth that homosexuals are unstable by portraying gay characters as somehow troubled.

Where are the portrayals of healthy, well-rounded lesbian and gay individuals? Where are the depictions of loving and caring lesbian and gay parents, gay psychologists, nurses, social workers, doctors, teachers, etc.?

We must continue to challenge the media to address their heterosexism. And, at the same time, we must continue to be visible in our ordinary, daily lives so that we can help others see beyond these stereotypes.

I'd long since accepted the fact that nothing had ever happened to me and nothing ever would. That's how the closet feels, once you have made your nest in it and learned to call it home, self-pity becomes your oxygen.

Paul Monette
writer

Sometimes we delay our coming out to wait for the most "opportune time" to do so. And that time never seems to come. There's always some excuse as to why we didn't come out to a friend, family member or co-worker. What have we gained by this delay? Probably nothing. What have we lost? We've lost a piece of our pride, and many missed opportunities to share our life more fully with those close to us. We've lost a chance to heal by being honest with others about who we really are.

You can't turn back the clock. So take your next step in healing today.

[On quilt panel commemorating his death]:
I came here today to ask that this nation with all its resources and compassion not let my epitaph read he died of red tape.

Roger Lyon
AIDS activist

The gay community has led this country's response to the AIDS epidemic. The government's slow and ineffective response to this epidemic is a disgrace to the nation. It is a crime so many people have needlessly died. It is a disgrace because these deaths are tied to Americans' contempt for gays.

Lesbians and gays will continue to be in the forefront of advancing change as we wait for other humanitarian leaders to stand up and speak loudly about the injustices our community endures. Take pride in the many lesbian and gay leaders we have who persist in speaking up even when others may not want to listen. Our voices cannot be ignored.

It was inevitable that outrageousness exploded with the beginnings of gay liberation. Hooray for sassy risk and silly experiment and anarchic joy!

James Broughton
poet

Sometimes being conventional just doesn't get the point across. "Sassy risk" certainly has it's role in helping people see their prejudicial views of lesbians and gays. For example, ACT UP (AIDS Coalition To Unleash Power) certainly played a helpful role in responding to the AIDS epidemic. And the "kiss ins," staged by Queer Nation, increased lesbian and gay visibility.

The conventional and the sassy both have their role. Do your part, however you choose. Just do it!

It's only when we truly know and understand that we have a limited time on earth—and that we have no way of knowing when our time is up—that we begin to live each day to the fullest, as if it was the only one we had.

Elisabath Kübler-Ross
author

We know, yet we forget. Do we sometimes forget we have a limited time on this earth because it's easier to go through the motions of day-to-day life than it is to make the changes we want in our lives? Our forgetfulness may be our procrastination or fear of change.

You have the power to make changes in your life today. Stop procrastinating. Start by finding one thing you want to change—now.

We have mountains to move, and we have, today, only our hands to move them with. But every day there are more hands.

Rita Mae Brown
writer

Growing up lesbian or gay we had few hands to hold to guide us. Fortunately this is changing. Our lesbian and gay sisters and brothers are more visible and more accessible. Our heterosexual friends are joining hands.

If you feel alone, reach out for a helping hand. If you have support, extend a helping hand. We are truly building bridges.

As hidden as you have been from others, that is how hidden you have been from yourself.

Sally Fisher
educator/writer
AIDS Mastery Workshop

I almost hesitate to call our process of acknowledging and accepting our homosexuality as "coming out." We would not go through this painful struggle if we had not been ostracized and shamed by society. Somehow, by referring to it as our "coming out process" it seems to imply that it's part of being homosexual. Our coming out process isn't because we're homosexual, it's because we've been victimized. There's a big difference.

Let's take the onus off of us and identify our struggle for what it is: healing from cultural victimization. We live in a culture that has taught us to hide and deny our very being. We no longer need to hide.

MAY 31

The walls of the closet are guarded by the dogs of terror, and inside of the closet is a house of mirrors.

Judy Grahn
writer

The closet takes its toll. The fear immobilizes us. Personal growth is stunted. Hiding is an attempt to protect ourselves. But can we ultimately protect ourselves by staying in the closet? Can change occur when our voices remain unheard? The answer is no.

Free your voice. When you do so your fear will subside.

*Life is either a daring adventure or nothing.
To keep our faces toward change and behave
like free spirits in the presence of fate is
strength undefeatable.*

Helen Keller

We draw strength and wisdom from others who have struggled. We have been able to periodically retreat from our struggles because we can conceal our homosexuality. We must not falter by hiding too long. Sitting in the "safety" and "comfort" of the closet too long brings stagnation and death of the spirit.

We must continue to come out in whatever ways are possible. To come out is to live life fully.

this man, if you could see him as I do
from the kitchen door
in secret, like a cat,
is love in flesh and bone
for all his giving

Boyer Rickel
poet

The loving and giving between lesbian and gay partners goes unnoticed by those who refuse to see it and those who have been conditioned not to see it, even when it stares them in the face. What beauty and love they miss!

We see it. We know it. We feel it. We also need to celebrate and nurture the love that enriches our lives.

After you have mastered the discomfort of hiding, why not come out and risk having what you want?

Sally Fisher
educator/writer
AIDS Mastery Workshop

Letting go of the shame can take a lifetime of work. The longer we are isolated, the longer we remain subjected to negative, shaming messages about homosexuality. Our process of releasing the shame is related to the duration and severity of our victimization.

Support and understanding from others helps us let go of our sense of being "outcasts." With understanding from just a few others, we can release our feelings of being outcasts even if others in society persist in seeing us as such.

Have you found the support you need and deserve? It's out there. Reach out.

What I will never forgive is your daring to try and make me ashamed of my love. I'm not ashamed of it, there's no shame in me.

Radclyffe Hall
novelist

Release the shame and reclaim your pride. Refusing to be shamed any longer is an indication of your self-acceptance and burgeoning self-confidence. We not only refuse to buy into the shaming messages, but we express our anger and indignation when the shaming stereotypes are presented.

Although our pride develops from within as we release the shame, it is bolstered when we take action.

Something of exquisite beauty arose in the mind of each at last, something unforgettable and eternal, but built of the humblest scraps of speech and from the simplest emotions.

"I say, will you kiss me?" asked Maurice, when the sparrows woke in the eaves above them, and far out in the woods the ringdoves began to coo.

E.M. Forster
author

It's essential to continue to release our shame of being homosexual so that it does not interfere with our relationships with lovers and significant others. If one person hides in the shadow of the closet while the other's spirit flies free, the pleasures of loving and living get muddled and stifled.

Lacking self-love, we may search for a relationship in the hopes that "if someone else loves me, I must be okay." Love yourself first. Everything else will follow naturally.

JUNE 6

Our silence will not protect us.

Audre Lorde
writer

The safety of the closet is only temporary at best. The initial sense of safety in the closet is only an illusion. Continued silence results in suffocating ourselves within the closet. Or someone else will already know we're hiding in the closet and throw open the doors.

We protect ourselves best by breaking the silence. Breaking the silence restores self-esteem and self-confidence. Our best protection is our pride and resilience!

The power of change lies with you.

Steve Endean
founder
Human Rights Campaign Fund

It is common for people who have been victimized (and all lesbians and gays have been culturally victimized in our society) to develop a sense of hopelessness about their future. On one hand, this hopelessness may be a tremendous despair that immobilizes oneself. Or, equally devastating but less obvious, this hopelessness may take a more subtle form of passivity, such as feelings that other people and events control your life. These feelings are the result of victimization.

To take back your power, you must realize that change needs to *and can* come from within.

Insanity is doing the same thing over and over again, but expecting different results.

Rita Mae Brown
writer

We take the same steps within the confining walls of the closet over and over so that they become familiar. We misinterpret familiarity as comfortability. It's our own participation in insanity; the insanity that festers and builds within the closet.

The insanity becomes clear as years in the closet breed a suffocation that we can no longer deny. Or the insanity is unveiled after we step out of the closet. Choose the latter.

[In response to President Clinton's failure to lift the ban on gays in the military]: *If you want to change the world, don't rely on others.*

Tim McFeeley
executive director
Human Rights Campaign Fund

We can ask for help. We can demand change. But, ultimately, for change to occur, we must do it ourselves. A lot of well-intentioned people do not fully understand the issues facing lesbians and gays. And oftentimes their support crumbles when pressured by others.

We not only can make changes, we must take responsibility for making the changes we see necessary. The power lies within each of us. Access it! Use it!

Coming out is just the first step, the outer coming out. Then we have to start the inner coming out, looking to nourish our own battered self-esteem.

Paul Monette
writer

The acknowledgment of who we are is the first step in a lifelong process of accepting and celebrating one's homosexuality. Lesbians and gays may acknowledge their homosexuality without consciously examining how heterosexism has battered their self-esteem.

It makes sense that as children we learn to say, "I'm not going to let that bother me" and then keep our pain at a distance because we have no one to talk to about our homosexuality. As adults this is no longer effective.

In fact, keeping our pain at bay hinders our development of close interpersonal relationships. We must first talk about our pain, and how our self-esteem has been battered so that we can move on to celebrating our gayness.

There never was night that had no morn.

Dinah Mulock Craik
poet

To lose hope is to stay frightened in the night. The pain, the prejudice and the abuse we suffer fosters this loss of hope. But hope does remain. A new morning does approach.

As the numbers at the March on Washington in 1979, 1987 and 1993 attest, lesbians and gays coming out, demanding justice and reclaiming their pride are multiplying rapidly.

Celebrate with the numbers! Move out of the dark.

I am glad to be gay because in spite of all the adversities, it is more interesting to see the world without the blinders worn by those who subscribe to cultural myths like the inevitability of the nuclear family, the brutality of men, and the necessity of greed and war and histories written in endlessly flowing blood.

Arnie Kantrowitz
writer

Lesbians and gays have been forced into an "outsiders" role in society. As we have challenged that role, we have also embraced it. Being able to look at society from the outsider perspective provides insights about the human condition, and insights that provide fuel for change.

Adversity to insight. Insight to change. Are you stuck? Or are you choosing to benefit from the "outsiders" role?

Why can't people go to any bookstore and go buy gay books? They should be able to. On the other hand, straight society is not going to preserve gay culture. So, we'll do it ourselves.

Neil Woodward
founder
Category Six, Denver's first
gay and lesbian bookstore

From oral to written history, the lesbian and gay community is truly "making history." Most school curricula fail to mention the contributions of lesbians and gays. We ask "Where is the chapter on lesbians and gays throughout history?"

Whereas heterosexual historians have presented a straight and narrow perspective, lesbians and gays are reclaiming our historical past. We are rewriting history so that future generations will clearly recognize our contributions.

This time . . .
I'm gonna love myself
More than anyone else.

Tracy Chapman
singer/songwriter

Neediness develops from deprivation. Deprived of the love, care and respect we deserve as lesbians and gays, we reach adulthood sometimes clinging to relationships because of our own unmet emotional needs. We look toward others to enrich our lives and "make us whole." Most of our energy goes toward loving and caring for them, and we forget to love ourselves. We fail to realize that no one can "fix" those unmet needs except ourselves.

Refocus on validation from within. Refocus on self love. Love yourself so that love between you and others is not stifling but healthy and fulfilling.

I know what you must be thinking now. You're asking yourself: What did we do wrong? . . . I can't answer that, Mama. In the long run, I guess I really don't care. All I know is this: If you and Papa are responsible for the way I am, then I thank you with all my heart, for it's the light and the joy of my life.

Armistead Maupin
writer

Have you thanked your parents for the gift of homosexuality? If not, why? Is it because after years of hearing negative myths about homosexuality that even you don't see it as a gift? Then it's time to re-examine.

Your homosexuality is a gift. Your challenge is to recognize it and embrace it.

It's exhilarating to be alive in a time of awakening consciousness; it can also be confusing, disorienting and painful.

Adrienne Rich
poet

Making history brings joy and pain. We make history daily by living our lives as "out" lesbians and gays. Being out has a multitude of rewards and accompanying challenges. And what makes it all worthwhile? It's not the joy and pain, it's the sense of pride we capture only by facing the challenge of being true to ourselves.

It's so easy for people to harbor prejudices when they are only dealing with faceless stereotypes and soulless statistics. It is much harder for them to maintain fears and suspicions when the statistic is revealed to be the trusted neighbor or the respected colleague, and the stereotype doesn't fit the school principal or the corporate executive.

Carlos Stelmach
magazine editor-in-chief

Our secrecy perpetuates the myth that lesbians and gays are perverse or sick. When responsible and respected individuals identify themselves as lesbian or gay, bigots are forced to examine their prejudices. They can no longer profess that all lesbians and gays fit the stereotypes they grew up with. From the average person, our coming out will bring words of support and a greater willingness to understand us as fellow human beings.

We can pick who we call our friends!

No one can make you feel inferior without your consent.

Eleanor Roosevelt

As you release the shaming messages about homosexuality you grew up with, you loosen the power others hold over you. Our self-confidence suffers as we are oppressed.

Our oppressors would like us to perpetuate self-hatred, because then they maintain their power over us. It's difficult to stand up for oneself when we're filled with self-hate.

Take back your power. Let go of the negative messages. Celebrate being gay!

There are some things you learn best in calm, and some in storm.

Willa Cather
writer

Lessons about equality and justice are learned in storms. When lesbians and gays have been under attack by psychiatrists, the military or religious institutions, they have responded with a fury of demands for justice.

We learn that the rights we should be able to take for granted are instead the ones we must fight for vehemently. However, we also learn the necessity of fighting for basic human rights for all individuals, and to take pride in who we are. The storms have made us a stronger and more courageous community.

....

Loneliness is the poverty of self; solitude is the richness of self.

May Sarton
poet

One of the effects of victimization is insecurity that results in difficulty being alone with oneself. We have difficulty being alone because we think we need validation from others.

We must learn to embrace periods of solitude. Solitude is a time for personal reflection and growth. As we learn to validate ourselves from within, we learn to appreciate the richness of solitude.

Till it has loved, no man or woman can become itself.

Emily Dickenson
poet

The giving of love is the very expression of our humanness. Lesbians and gays are told they are incapable of loving. We all know this is not true. What is true is that when we internalize shaming messages about our homosexuality, these messages interfere with our ability to love others. This happens because our shame first interferes with our ability to love *ourselves.*

To give love fully, we must release the shaming myths about homosexuality. Then we will love ourselves, and can love others unencumbered.

Until the lie of hatred and bigotry is over-come . . . by the Truth of Love and Acceptance.

The Living Earth Art Project
at the 1993 March on Washington

The lesbian and gay civil rights movement is not just about securing equal rights. It's also about pointing our finger and saying "Hatred and bigotry have got to go!"

For years bigots have been saying homosexuals need to change. We now say, "It's time for *you* to change."

Stop hatred, not homosexuality. We now take the burden off of our shoulders and place it where it belongs. Our movement challenges the world to stop hate and to love instead. The challenge can no longer go unnoticed, as our expressions of love and compassion expose the hatred of others.

Gay people don't know their history . . . At a certain age we discover we're gay and suddenly we don't have connections anymore. The institutions we grow up with—our churches, schools, families—don't give us a sense of culture or history as gay people. We have to invent it each time we come out.

Chuck Forester
co-chair
Gay and Lesbian Center
of the new San Francisco Public Library

Lesbians and gays have the unique challenge of creating our own rituals and celebrations that help define our culture. Unique in the sense that we have been rejected by the larger culture; their norms do not apply.

We only have to look at the many ways we honor and celebrate our relationships. This is our chance to be creative and not to be hindered by pre-existing cultural norms!

Suddenly, we really are everywhere: on the cover of Time *magazine, on "Good Morning America," on* C-Span, *and in the "Letters to the editor" of daily newspapers, no matter how tiny the town.*

C.J. Janovy
journalist

Lesbian and gay visibility has arrived. And from where has it come? It started as a tiny ripple in the 1960s when a small but growing number of lesbians and gays came out of the closet. That ripple has turned into a powerful wave as more and more come out.

You have the opportunity to "catch the wave." The power of change is embedded in our willingness to come out.

[In response to right-wing attacks on her book *Heather Has Two Mommies*]: *People talk about family values. In my book, the teacher tells Heather that the most important thing about a family is that all people in it love each other. Like that's such a horrendous message to be spreading? The right-wing opponents of the book said it was propaganda.*

Leslea Newman
author

Any message may be seen as propaganda. However, we get to decide what messages we want to pass on to our children. Those messages can be filled with hate or love.

The messages from bigots are clearly filled with hate. Messages of tolerance and acceptance are based on love.

I am proud to be a gay man because I have the freedom to act outside of accepted and destructive roles of male behavior.

John G.

Heterosexual norms have fostered the belief that being male means being masculine, and that being female means embracing all things feminine. Masculinity is valued and femininity is devalued; hence, males perpetuate their "superiority" over women. What nonsense and how oppressive! We still have much work to do to combat these sexist stereotypes.

Thankfully, it is a growing number of lesbian and gay people who, by embracing both their masculinity and femininity, are challenging these harmful stereotypes. It is a clear reminder of how sexism and heterosexism are interrelated.

Celebrate your femininity and masculinity!

[Letter to Ann and Alfred Corn]: *Well, the big news here is Gay Power. It's the most extraordinary thing. It all began two weeks ago on a Friday night. The cops raided the Stonewall. . . .*

Edmund White
author

Visibility is power. Remember the power of our visibility when we finally took a stand at Stonewall. Many Americans actually believe they don't know any lesbians and gays. Underestimates of our numbers, such as the report claiming 1% of the population is gay, are only reinforced when we remain invisible. If every lesbian and gay in this country came out to a new person every year, within five to ten years everyone in the country would outwardly know someone who is lesbian or gay.

Coming out is an ongoing life process. Don't stop now when the steps that each one of us take have such impact on so many others! Let the power of Stonewall live on.

I think that one thing our enemies will never understand . . . is that the harder they try to push us back into the closet, the more outpouring there's going to be. . . . By trying to repress us, they really bring out the militancy in us and make for a lot more visible gay people.

Jean O'Leary
former co-executive director
National Lesbian and Gay Task Force (NLGTF)

In past decades it was more difficult to stay visible. At this point in time, lesbians and gays have formed every kind of organization imaginable—political, social, athletic, academic and so on. We continue to be more visible. The sense of pride and personal power that comes from this visibility is the fuel that easily ignites when attempts to silence us occur.

The lesbian and gay civil rights movement cannot be stopped. As our pride grows, so does our power.

I wish more prominent people could bring themselves to come out of their closets. Nearly always the world knows who they are already, however hard they try to fool it. Coming out would actually make their lives less isolated and troubled; it would give them faith and courage in themselves. And isn't that worth far more than the notoriety they already enjoy?

Christopher Isherwood
writer

Each of us, no matter how well known we are, make decisions about whether or not to come out. Prominent individuals can help lead the way by being courageous. As we have seen in recent years when famous individuals conceal their homosexuality, it is usually revealed in unpleasant terms upon their death.

Our decisions about coming out determine how we will be known in life and in death, whether we'll be respected or scorned.

No matter how far in or out of the closet you are—you have a next step.

ad slogan at the 1987
March on Washington

Coming out is a lifelong process, not a one-time occurrence. Whether you're just coming out to yourself or continuing to come out to new friends, it goes on and on. What starts out as a painful and fearful process is eventually transformed to continuing acts of empower-ment. Fear is transformed to pride.

We reclaim our pride with each step. Keep walking.

*We [lesbians and gays] are not in the habit
of thinking of ourselves as leading our civilization, and yet we do.*

Judy Grahn
writer

Lesbians and gays are leaders. Leaders,
because we challenge society to look at their
inhumanity. Leaders, because in spite of all the
obstacles we face we learn to love ourselves.
We build healthy, productive lives. And, we do
more: we reach out and give back to the same
society that has turned its back on us.

Take pride in being part of a courageous,
spirited, giving and compassionate community. By taking care of yourself, you show the
world that you are a leader.

Oppression can only survive through silence.

Carmen De Monteflores
writer

When each of us breaks the silence about the pain and suffering we have endured as lesbian and gay people living in a hostile world, the face of inhumanity is exposed. By sharing our stories and telling others what it was like growing up gay, our reality is voiced and validated. If not validated by others initially, at least validated by ourselves because we have spoken up.

When we speak up, we heal; for the message to ourselves and others is that we will stand up for ourselves, confronting the oppression we face. We can move from victim to survivor, and from silence to action.

Whatever the state of our "gay pride," our politeness sticks to us all. It oozes from a well of acquiescence deep within, down where we still can't quite believe that we're as good as straights.

Darrel Yates Rist
writer

Discrimination of lesbians and gays promotes the harmful notion that we're second class. And what do we know about how people who have been victimized tend to act? They tend to be passive, silent and polite. They tend to make sure everyone else is okay at a great emotional cost to themselves.

Is your "politeness" tied to the victimization you have suffered? Do you show a polite exterior when inside you're burning with hurt and anger?

Put your needs first. Talk about your hurt and anger. It's okay to be angry. It's important to be assertive, not polite.

The thing about freedom, though, is that you can't just want it for yourself, or only for your own kind. Freedom means everybody.

Mab Segrest
author

There may be different struggles, but it is all part of the same fight. As we come out and dismantle the prejudice and oppression we have endured, it is important that we take care not to take the pain of our oppression out on others different than ourselves. Remember: prejudice hurts. Also remember: oppression is abuse.

To each of us, there are many people in this world different from ourselves. If we think we have healed yet continue to oppress others, healing has not happened. We must respect differences. We must value differences. This is what we're asking from others, so let's expect it from ourselves.

To love oneself is the beginning of a lifelong romance.

Oscar Wilde
writer

Being shamed about our homosexuality as we are growing up results in looking to others for validation. We doubt ourselves and look to others to say to us "you're okay." Instead, the validation needs to come from within ourselves. When we base our self-esteem on others' perceptions, we give them all the power.

Reclaim your power. Look within. Rediscover the love you have for yourself. The self-love that has been there all along, but was hidden away.

If the 1980s was the decade of coming out, the 1990s is the decade of coming home.

Torie Osborn
former executive director
National Lesbian and Gay Task Force (NLGTF)

We are coming home to our families across America as out and proud lesbians and gays. By the year 2000 no American will be able to claim "I don't know anyone who is lesbian or gay."

The marches on Washington, Gay Pride Day Parades, National Coming Out Day events and thousands of other gay events across the country help us to come out. The power we reclaim as participants in these events is brought back to our homes. The power is seen in the increasing number of lesbians and gays who are out to more and more people in their lives.

Get involved in a Gay Pride event. Reclaim your power and pride!

I wish that homosexuals were born with a little horn in the middle of their forehead so we couldn't hide so easily. At least if you can't hide, you have to stand up and fight.

Harvey Fierstein
actor/playwright

More lesbians and gays are proclaiming their homosexuality with pink triangles than ever before. Look at the backpacks and jackets we wear. Look at the pink triangles on cars and trucks across America.

We are less fearful. We are bolder. We are reclaiming our pride and letting America know we're here to stay and we're not going to hide.

Wear a pink triangle. Show your pride!

....

Some Reagan Administration supporters have gone on record as saying that AIDS is God's judgment on homosexuals, but you have never heard one of them say that Legionnaire's Disease was God's judgment on the right-wing views of the American Legion.

H. Carl McCall
chairman
New York State Division of Human Rights

Bigots have tried to use God as a means to justify their oppression of all sorts of people—from Native Americans to African-Americans, and now lesbians and gays. Such rhetoric may appeal to the uneducated. We, however, don't buy it. It doesn't take much to see beyond the foolishness of their words.

Point out their foolishness. It may help others "get it." In time, history will clearly point out how foolish the bigots are.

The greatest obstacle that gay people have is their fear of rejection on account of homosexuality.

Harry Britt
former San Francisco city supervisor

Our fear of rejection is tied to looking to others for our own validation. Validation that needs to come from within oneself. After being shamed about our homosexuality we look to others for approval. The result: we confuse *wanting* with *needing* approval. We may desperately *want* approval from others, but as adults we do not *need* anyone's approval to get on with our lives.

As you become your own person, the fear of rejection subsides. You can stand on your own. Those people who love and accept you for who you are will stand by your side.

Gays are in the vanguard of that final divorce of sex from conventional notions of sin . . . if we can take sex out of the realm of sin altogether and see it as something else to do with personal relationships and ethics, then we can finally get around to another phase of Christianity that is long overdue. That phase is the one which deals with the question of sin as violence; sin as cruelty; sin as murder, war and starvation.

Anne Rice
writer

Gay people are not a threat to society; violence and hatred are. Teaching tolerance and respect is necessary for a humane world. When religious and other institutions use their power to perpetuate hatred we must challenge them to return to the underlying principles on which society's institutions are based: tolerance, respect, dignity and freedom for all.

Promote tolerance. Demand respect.

[In response to the Supreme Court decision that held intact Georgia's sodomy laws used to persecute gays.]: *Isn't it a violation of the Georgia sodomy law for the Supreme Court to have its head up its ass?*

letter from a reader
of *Playboy* magazine

As much as we would hope, justice is not guaranteed. Justice is fought for and won. It is why lesbians and gays must continue to fight for freedom; basic freedoms such as the right to life, liberty and the pursuit of happiness.

Our struggle will not end until we can be free to go about our daily lives without the fear of persecution for being who we are. The fight is long, but it is a worthy fight.

In the meantime, we must continue to demand justice. We can take pride in our demands for justice.

When the light went on in my head, I knew it was from God . . . God didn't deliver me from my sexuality. God delivered me from guilt and shame and gave me a sense of pride . . . my sexuality was a gift from God.

Carolyn Mobley
founder
African-American Lesbian/Gay Alliance

Without the support of traditional religious institutions, it has been a struggle for lesbians and gays to reclaim their spirituality. It has propelled us to truly examine our spirituality. Ours is not a "take for granted" church membership that mimics spirituality. Ours is a rebirth. A rebirth of spirit and soul.

Silence the shaming religious messages you grew up with. To reclaim your homosexuality is to reclaim your spirituality.

I got attacked . . . It's funny, those guys in the park wanted to bust my face . . . but their motive was not to make me this better activist . . . but instead, they sent an activist on her way. Some real good came of that. It changed my whole life.

Joyce Hunter
co-founder
Harvey Milk High School
for Lesbian and Gay Teens

The abuse we have suffered can propel us into action or leave us passive and helpless. What happens to our justified anger and rage? We must find healthy ways to deal with it or it stays buried inside to stymie our growth. We have been abused too much already. To hold our anger inside is to brutalize ourselves once more.

Find a constructive way to release your anger. Make it work *for* you, not against you.

I am proud to be a gay man because I have been created by the same God who made all living things in tender and magnificent love.

John G.

Each individual—gay, straight, bisexual, transgender—is a work of art. Celebrating one's being is not limited to heterosexual individuals.

Society has tried to condition us to believe that homosexuality is a choice, and that heterosexuality is the only pure form of being.

When we begin to accept and celebrate what every individual has to offer, we will then be able to see that it is foolish to say that "God bestows his gifts on only select individuals (i.e., heterosexuals)." In fact, our gayness is a gift from God.

When I think of the "buddies" at Gay Men's Health Crisis and the volunteers at similar groups all over the country . . . I am sad and angry and glad to be gay because I belong to a people who will survive, no matter what befalls them.

Arnie Kantrowitz
writer

Many lesbian and gay people have not taken the time to think about why they are glad to be gay. After being taught absolutely no positives about being gay, many of us even wonder if there are any reasons to be glad to be gay.

Look around you. There are plenty of reasons to be glad to be gay. There are many reasons to be proud. Are you just "okay" with being gay or are you really proud?

There are many lesbians and gay men trapped by their fear into silence and invisibility, and they exist in a dim valley of terror wearing nooses of conformity. And for them, also, I ask your understanding . . . conformity is very seductive, as it is destructive and can also be a terrible and painful prison.

Audre Lorde
writer

Heterosexism has built the prisons within which we reside. But who will free us? Only we can free our minds and spirits. And only upon freeing our minds and spirits can we challenge the heterosexism that continues to force our sisters and brothers into the closet.

Don't give up on freeing your spirit, for heterosexism is a bit like chess. It can seem like checkmate when it's only check. There are many more moves left in this game which you have only just begun to play.

For love and for life . . . we are not going back.

slogan at the
1987 March on Washington

At the 1987 March on Washington over 600,000 of us—lesbians, gays and our friends—marched to show the world our existence and that we're not going away. Washington had never seen a march so large. Yet the National Park Service estimated a fraction of our number and the media ignored us.

Then in 1993 at the third March on Washington, a million people showed that we're certainly not going back into the closet. We can no longer be ignored. The media is finally taking note.

We demand to have our lives acknowledged and respected. This is a fight for love and for life.

JULY 18

Some people become heroic on the grand scale—Harvey Milk, for instance. Yet the rest of us are no less heroic when we pick a place to stand and refuse to budge. Each time we make that moral stand, we change history.

Yvonne Bergquist
writer

Everyday hero . . . yes, you! Each time you stand up for yourself as a lesbian or gay man in spite of the discrimination and prejudice we face you change history. Sometimes we forget to give ourselves credit for taking a stand.

Being out is taking a stand on a daily basis. Take time to pat yourself on the back. You deserve it, you're an everyday hero!

The time is coming soon
When the blind remove their blinders
And the speechless speak the truth.

Tracy Chapman
singer/songwriter

Oppression, seemingly formidable, also has numbered days because the collective human spirit is all enduring and eventually the voices of the oppressed will be raised and heard. For lesbian and gay people, that time is now.

For whatever reasons, our voices resonate across this country. Individuals, like you and me, far and near share the truths of our victimization. Our plight will be known. And our healing begins.

JULY 20

When I think of the federal gay and lesbian civil rights bills, it no longer seems irrelevant or farfetched, but historically inevitable.

John D'Emilio
gay historian

With the barriers we still face, we sometimes forget to stand back and put our struggle in an historical context. We have made numerous advances in gay liberation in the last 25 years. The Stonewall riots in 1969 to one million lesbians and gays marching on Washington in 1993. In the 1960s it was rare to see the media talk about homosexuals and most gays didn't feel safe to come out of the closet.

Now, millions of lesbians and gays are out of the closet. It's hard to pick up a publication that doesn't have a story about us!

No, the struggle is not over, nor will it end with the passage of a federal civil rights bill. But we are moving forward and nothing can stop us now.

The voice is a wild thing. It can't be bred in captivity.

Willa Cather
writer

Lesbians and gays will no longer be silenced. We realize the power of our courageous voices. Look around you. Whereas 20 and 30 years ago it was difficult to hear our voices expressed, we now see lesbians and gays writing their own histories, creating their own music, establishing libraries, bookstores, magazines and newspapers across the country.

Lift your voice. Our once timid voices grow louder. How will you let your voice be heard?

Old memories are so empty when they cannot be shared.

Jewelle Gomez
writer

We establish families in part to share our stories and pass on our traditions. Sometimes lesbians and gays grow up believing they cannot have family because that's what they were taught to believe. Lesbians and gays have always been part of families, they just haven't been as visible as other families.

In recent years we find many courageous lesbian and gay families going public stating "We are family, too!" We *are* family.

We must take the responsibility to create our own family, however we define it, to ensure that we nurture and care for ourselves and our loved ones—something that others have tried to deny us for all too long.

When you are intimate with yourself you can see through the veil of amnesia and recognize who you are on the deepest level.

Sally Fisher
educator/writer
AIDS Mastery Workshop

Coming to grips with our homosexuality isn't just about sex. Initially, the focus may be on an unleashed sexual and romantic freedom toward persons of our same sex. But ultimately, gay liberation is about human liberation— that each of us might be intimate with ourselves and others and develop our own individual talents, realize our own dreams, establish our own families and be all that we can be without prejudice and pressure to conform to something we are not.

Gay liberation is a journey of self-discovery.

I like the word gay, though I think of myself more as queer. I believe the strength in my work comes from that perspective—my being an outsider.

Holly Hughes
playwright

Homosexual, lesbian, gay, dyke, fag or queer—which word describes us best? In some ways it's unfortunate we have to have labels to help define ourselves. But after hundreds of years of attempts to silence lesbians and gays, the language we choose to define ourselves has powerful implications for our visibility and survival. Which word we choose is not as important as the meaning the word has for us.

Choose a word and use it with the power of affirmation. Then the label acknowledges us and is used to reclaim our specialness and our pride.

Why we are Negroes, Jews or homosexuals is totally irrelevant, and whether we can be changed to whites, Christians or heterosexuals is equally irrelevant.

Frank Kameny
co-founder
Mattachine Society of Washington, D.C.

Attempts to answer the question why we are lesbian or gay is rooted in society's heterosexism and homophobia. It's based on the assumption that the only way to be is heterosexual. That it is more "natural" to be heterosexual than homosexual. The bigotry is clear. As long as there have been people on this earth some have always been homosexual. This will be true as long as there are humans on this planet. Acceptance of this reality is the real issue.

By challenging the heterosexism involved in attempting to answer why we are gay, we confront the blatant bigotry at hand.

What we have to acknowledge is that our own passivity has given the opposition a free rein to be the loudest voices . . . We are the last acceptable prejudice, and we've got to say that intolerance is intolerable.

Virginia Apuzzo
former director
National Lesbian and Gay Task Force (NLGTF)

Speaking up is part of healing from the negative effects of heterosexism. Remaining silent and passive keeps us in the role of the victim. To heal is to become a survivor. To become a survivor we must speak up about the injustices we face. By doing so we reclaim our power. We let others know we will no longer be walked on. This is how we reclaim our pride.

The very fact that our laws make homosexuality a crime puts the stamp of approval on the idea that "queers" are animals . . . The society's values make the homosexual a "faggot," easy prey . . .

Dr. John Money
sexologist
Johns Hopkins University

Society is responsible for the violence lesbians and gays face. Teaching children to devalue homosexuality perpetuates hatred toward homosexuals. Hence, the violence is predictable, but nonetheless reprehensible.

Since society is slow to educate children about positive images of homosexuality, we must do so. By being out and proud gay individuals we can teach young children to respect us, not hate us.

Stop the violence by being out. Being out helps eliminate hatred and teaches respect. Kids need it and so do we.

One time when my Ma wondered how come I turned out gay, I asked her, "Ma, how come my brothers didn't?"

Sal Mineo
actor

Some people are clamoring to find out "what causes homosexuality" while failing to ask "what causes heterosexuality?" The bias is clear. Growing up with all the bias and prejudice, many lesbians and gays start to ask themselves the same question—sometimes looking for a "cure," hoping then to "fit in."

We don't need a cure for homosexuality any more than we do for heterosexuality. But we do need a cure for heterosexism and homophobia.

Remember: Homosexuality is natural. Bigotry is pathological.

If lesbians were purple, none would be admitted to respectful places. But if all lesbians suddenly turned purple today, society would be surprised at the number of purple people in high places.

Sidney Abbott and Barbara Love
authors

In the 1990s, a growing number of lesbians and gays are being admitted to "respectable places." Take for instance, President Clinton's appointment of openly lesbian Roberta Achtenberg.

At the same time, there are still many lesbians and gays hiding in the closet. Remember, coming out is a lifelong process.

Take your next step in coming out. To avoid doing so is to stop growing. Each time we come out we reclaim a bit of pride. Each time we come out we heighten someone else's awareness of the reality that *we are everywhere.*

Say one thing, do another. Tell them what they want to hear. It would be years, however, before Carol discovered where their indoctrination ended and her own thinking began.

Randy Shilts
journalist/author

Leading a double life results in a loss of self. We spend years of practice saying one thing to others while believing something else, and even *we* become confused. Who is the real me? Where do I start and the voices of others stop?

Perhaps over time we no longer see the "Catch 22" we have been forced into. We become the voice of others without knowing.

Finding yourself is finding your own voice. Take time to ask yourself, "After all the indoctrination, who is the real me?"

Now we've gone back to our individual lives. Perhaps it is time to let those around us know the faces that were in the crowd that Sunday in Washington. We can encourage social change simply by demystifying ourselves as lesbians and gays for people we know, one at a time.

Carlos Stelmach
magazine editor-in-chief

The daughter of a woman I work with brought a friend into the office one day. After visiting with her mother, her friend said "I know you work with gay people, I would like to meet one. I don't know any." I introduced myself as a gay person. I felt like a novelty item. Afterwards, I realized we cease being novelty items, or people to fear, only when they know us as humans.

To demystify ourselves, we must come out. Who is the next person you are willing to share your "humanness" with?

No government has the right to tell its citizens when or whom to love. The only queer people are those who don't love anybody.

Rita Mae Brown
writer

Love takes many forms. Attempts to legislate love will continue to fail because there are as many forms of loving as there are individuals. Loving only becomes political when the fearful and bigoted impose their rigid beliefs of "good love" and "bad love." Legislation does not stop loving.

To love is a personal act. Express your love. To deny our love is to deny our humanness.

We must be the last generation to live in silence.

Paul Monette
writer

Too much pain and suffering have been endured by countless lesbians and gays for many generations. We must be the last generation to live in silence because we now have the power to make changes. We have growing support from many understanding heterosexual friends and family who are willing to speak up about the abuses lesbians and gays suffer. We must seize these opportunities so that future generations of lesbians and gays will not suffer needlessly.

Think back to the support you lacked as a child and how affirming it would have been to have lesbian and gay role models to look up to.

By celebrating your gayness, and being open about yourself, you will give hope to someone younger who is desperately looking for positive images of what it means to be gay.

That (a self-proclaimed homosexual) was named to the Criminal Court of New York City says, as it should to young gay people, that they can be who they are, that they do not have to dissemble about what they are, and that they can also achieve whatever their abilities will allow them to do.

Richard C. Failla
American judge

All the shaming myths about homosexuality will not stifle us. As children we doubted our potential because we were told that all lesbians and gays were despicable, self-loathing and could not be happy and successful.

Our visibility today decreases the impact of these shaming messages for younger lesbians and gays. A new generation of lesbians and gays already takes pride in their homosexuality. For this generation, homosexuality is not a barrier to growth but a call for personal action.

The U.S. Olympics Committee singled out the Gay Olympics with a lawsuit prohibiting the use of the word "Olympics." They didn't sue the American Olympics, the Black Olympics, the Chinese Olympics . . . the USOC claims that it was a question of trademark law, not homophobia . . . Anyone who believes that must think that Rosa Park's struggle to sit where she wanted on a Montgomery bus was really about transit policy.

Art Agnos
former mayor of San Francisco

Attempts to mask discrimination by claiming other issues is an old trick. Though lesbians and gays may not "officially" proclaim a Gay "Olympics," many lesbians and gays informally refer to the Gay Games as the Gay Olympics in spite of the court decision.

We are able to see the truth. Time will place this injustice in proper perspective for all.

It is only too obvious that if help for civilization is ever to arrive, it will come not from the hands of those who, against all their instincts, have adapted themselves to the status quo but from those who by silent example have shown the world how to be more tolerant.

Quentin Crisp
writer

The push and pull of many factors creates change. Acceptance of homosexuality is coming about because of both political action and the quiet resolution of lesbians and gays who continue to live their lives as openly lesbian and gay individuals.

Change on the political level occurs slowly. There is an interplay of advances and setbacks for our rights. Politics, however, eventually catches up with the people.

It is the daily examples of loving and compassionate lesbians and gays that is the cornerstone of any other changes that do occur.

The Air Force pinned a medal on me for killing a man and discharged me for making love to one.

Leonard Matlovich
U.S. Air Force sergeant

Military madness—lesbians and gays continue to be oppressed and abused by the military. Some ask, "Why be part of a killing machine in the first place?" Others stress the need to eliminate discrimination in each and every institution.

The military has not been held accountable for their abuse of power. One need not look far to find sanctioned abuse of women, people of color, lesbians and gays. We must continue to demand that the military be held accountable for these actions.

As we wait for justice, we must remember the first step is in "breaking the silence" by continuing to speak up.

I am proud to be a gay man because I have the opportunity to define creative alternatives to accepted forms of family and parenting.

John G.

Lesbians and gay men need to take credit for our part in challenging society to look beyond the "traditional" family as the only acceptable form of family. It is not the structure but the quality of the relationships that define families. In fact, many times "traditional" family structures have not provided the basics (e.g., unconditional love, support, shelter, etc.), but instead have been abusive and harmful environments to grow up in.

Lesbians and gay men are teaching others that the quality of our relationships, the loving, tender, caring and nurturing we provide for our family members is truly indicative of what a family is meant to be, regardless of its form.

And from that moment on the brink of summer's end, no one would ever tell me again that men like me couldn't love.

Paul Monette
writer

We know that love, compassion and sex between two people of the same sex is natural. Politicians criminalized homosexuality out of fear, hatred and ignorance. Psychologists and psychiatrists such as Evelyn Hooker and Judd Marmor have tried for decades to push for greater understanding of lesbians and gays. You would think our country's leaders would take note. Unfortunately, many of our elected officials succumb to a vocal minority, and then fail to do their job: they fail to be effective and courageous leaders who promote justice and equality.

Though legislation lags behind social acceptance, don't let it keep you from loving. Celebrate who you are now. They'll catch up eventually.

Being gay has taught me tolerance, compassion and humility. It has shown me the limitless possibilities of living. It has given me people whose passion and kindness and sensitivity have provided a constant source of strength.

Armistead Maupin
writer

We have the opportunity to learn from the victimization we have suffered because we are lesbian and gay. The opportunity to learn that discrimination and prejudice toward individuals who are different from ourselves in any way, whether race, age, etc., is wrong, hurtful and abusive.

We have experienced the pain. Let's not inflict the pain on others. Instead, as we remember our pain, respond with the kindness and compassion we expect from others. Our example teaches others. Our example touches others.

All that you have is your soul.

Tracy Chapman
singer/songwriter

When you look at your life, how many things are you hanging on to that are keeping you from living your life the way you really want to as a lesbian or gay person? Are you spending more time and energy being someone you don't want to be or really being yourself? It might seem like an odd question, but sometimes we just "go through the motions" staying stuck, and in effect not really being happy with our lives.

Take time to find yourself. Don't try to separate your "gay" self. Integrate it into the whole.

Every out lesbian, gay and bi is a hero . . . Because, against all odds, we forge our identities. Because we nurture and protect and fight for one another. Because, in spite of everything we are told about ourselves, we are creative, productive and giving.

from the official program guide
for the 1993 March on Washington

Out lesbians and gays do mature into healthy, giving and compassionate individuals in spite of the shaming society we grow up in. Our resiliency is remarkable. Living one's life as an openly lesbian or gay individual is heroic and therefore reason for intense pride. Lesbians and gays still struggling in the closet recognize and want this pride.

Be out. By being out we help others come out and claim their pride.

I think in fifty years, when this catastrophe is all over, we will look back on this as our Holocaust; and we should feel the same anger that the survivors of the Holocaust still feel; and we should demand the same shame that the world should feel about the Holocaust.

Paul Monette
writer

Where is our anger? Our anger remains hidden behind our unresolved shame about our homosexuality. To express ourselves, to unleash our pain, outrage and anger, we must discard the shaming messages about homosexuality in our culture and reaffirm our pride in being gay.

Victims are stifled in raising their voices. It is the survivor, the empowered and the self-confident individual who speaks boldly. It is our voices that will let the truth be known. Raise your voice. Victims to survivors. Messengers of the truth.

I find pleasure in watching women in each other's arms, waltzing well.

Gabrielle Sidonie Colette
novelist

How many simple pleasures do you deny yourself because of the fear and shame you have internalized from a heterosexist society? Probably more than you realize. Think about those times you have deliberated about simple, natural things, like walking down the street hand in hand.

Lesbians and gays go through emotional gymnastics just to do the ordinary because we've been taught to believe that for *us* the ordinary does not exist. Continuing the emotional gymnastics is giving others too much power. We end up living life to please others rather than taking care of ourselves.

Taking back our power involves stopping the emotional gymnastics and people-pleasing. What are your needs? Start putting yourself first.

I have come to believe, over and over again, that what is most important to me must be spoken, made verbal and shared, even at the risk of having it bruised or misunderstood, that the speaking profits me, beyond any other effect . . .

Audre Lorde
writer

Sharing our stories makes healing possible. Holding in the pain of what it has been like growing up lesbian and gay is like the snow covering the vestiges of the previous summer. The flames of hope grow cold and are further buried. Our spring is breaking the silence and sharing our stories.

Healing begins by voicing the pain held within. Let the spring that follows the winter begin.

Silence = Death

slogan used by ACT UP
(AIDS Coalition to Unleash Power)

The AIDS epidemic challenged the gay community to face the fact that staying silent and staying in the closet made us accomplices to the oppression we endure. In the case of AIDS, our silence was not merely a stumbling block in attempts to hasten the fight, our silence was literally killing us.

With virtually no concerted response from the larger community, the gay community realized that it couldn't afford to wait for others to speak up for us. The AIDS epidemic has moved our community from: Silence = Death to: Action = Power.

Too frequently lesbians and gays in their coming out process see their negative self-concept as a result of their homosexuality rather than as a result of their victimization.

Joseph Neisen

One stereotype we grow up with about homosexuals is that lesbians and gays are inherently self-loathing and filled with self-hate. Wrong! Our self-hate is not because we're gay. Rather, it's because we've been victimized by a heterosexist society.

When we are inundated from birth with harmful, shaming and erroneous messages about homosexuality, it's not surprising we reach our teen years wondering if maybe being homosexual is equated with being miserable. Let's put the blame where it belongs: on those individuals who perpetuated the harmful stereotypes. Stop blaming yourself, you've been victimized too long as it is!

I choose life . . .
Step out of the shadow of fear.

Rumors of The Big Wave Band
performed at the
1993 March on Washington

Coming out is stepping out of the shadow of fear. Coming out is choosing life, choosing to fully participate in life, choosing to live life with pride not shame.

The message repeated over and over by speakers at the 1993 March on Washington was clear: Come Out! Come out to others! Come out now! Who have you thought about coming out to and have procrastinated in doing so? What are you waiting for? "Step out of the shadow of fear." Choose life.

*If there is a faith that can move mountains,
it is faith in your own power.*

Marie von Ebner-Eschenbach

Our personal power and sense of pride
have been derided in this society that shames
us.

When we reclaim our pride as lesbians and
gays we restore our sense of personal power.
We *do* move mountains when our personal
power is restored.

All our dreams are possible when we maintain our pride. Take action on your dreams.

···

Just at a time when my personal gay activism is hitting a peak, I've come to the rather unsettling realization that my own homophobia is my biggest oppressor . . . Why do I sometimes kiss my lover, John, goodbye on the street and sometimes chicken out? Because I'm still trying to convince me *that it's okay to be gay.*

Rex Wockner
writer

Healing from the negative effects of heterosexism takes a long time. When the the shame that used to keep us down briefly returns, remember that you need not "beat yourself up." Others have done enough of this, you don't need to do more. Instead, recognize it as lingering shame, and then make a conscious choice about what you want to do with it.

If we periodically experience some shame, it does not mean we aren't healing. We only stop healing when we no longer make positive, conscious choices for ourselves.

He decided it was entirely possible that he was not the one who needed to change; it was society that did.

Randy Shilts
journalist/author

Oh, the power of the shaming cultural messages we have grown up with. Society teaches it is not okay to be gay and we make numerous attempts to comply. We learn to walk, talk and dress to pass as straight. Our thinking becomes chaotic as we try to learn how to pass and stay sane. We change as an attempt to save ourselves.

At some point we realize that our efforts to change for others are simply a crazy notion. We lose ourselves trying to please others.

Finding ourselves means we stop the charade. To stop the charade we must first recognize that we do not need to acquiesce. Instead, continue to remind yourself that it is society that needs to change.

I'm not afraid of storms, for I'm learning how to sail my ship.

Louisa May Alcott
author

The fear of rejection as we're on the brink of coming out, quickly subsides after the fact. And, why? Because we recognize we have reclaimed some of our pride after coming out.

Coming out is reclaiming pride. Coming out is regaining personal power.

How others respond suddenly becomes less important. Once the secrecy, the weight on our shoulders is removed, our world view changes. It is no longer clouded by trepidation of others, but fueled by self-confidence in finding our place in the world.

We render ourselves victims—depressed and powerless—when we don't trust ourselves, and consequently don't tell ourselves and others the truth about who we are. This is an expression of lack of self-respect, self-esteem, self-acceptance and self-love. It is also characteristic of life in the closet.

Rob Eichberg
author and co-founder
Experience Weekend

Begin with honesty. Self-respect is built on a foundation of honesty. We're taught to be dishonest with ourselves about being gay.

Acknowledging and accepting our homosexuality is simply being honest with ourselves and then others about who we are. Each time we're honest and open about being lesbian and gay, we foster our own pride.

Don't let others keep you from being honest about your own homosexuality. Choose honesty. Choose pride.

If I can stop one Heart from breaking,
I shall not live in vain
If I can ease one Life the Aching
Or cool one pain
Or help one fainting Robin
Unto his Nest again
I shall not live in vain.

Emily Dickinson
poet

The beauty of our community lies in the many ways we reach out to support each other when coming out and living our lives as proud lesbians and gays. A kind ear provides grateful support to someone struggling to rid themselves of the shaming messages they have internalized about homosexuality. Or a caring hand extended to show them a diverse and proud gay community is also supportive.

Sometimes these gestures get lost as we are more actively involved in making our voices heard. Take the hand of someone still struggling with self-acceptance. Keep sight of the kindness and love that has brought us together so that we might speak loudly.

Sometimes a person has to go back, really back—to have a sense, an understanding of all that's gone to make them—before they can go forward.

Paule Marshall

As children we learn to dissociate ourselves from the pain that comes from not being accepted as gay. It's a protective and helpful defense mechanism as a child.

However, as adults, it's vital to re-examine the pain we endured as children to help us "reconnect ourselves." To deny one's pain is to deny the opportunity to fully heal.

Share your stories. Share your pain. It allows the healing to happen.

If AIDS has taught us anything, it is that we are the most tenacious, inspired, creative, committed survivors on the face of this earth.

Roger McFarlane
former executive director
Gay Men's Health Crisis

The gay community's tenacity and resourcefulness is evidenced by the response to the AIDS epidemic. While the rest of the world ignored AIDS, the gay community mobilized to provide the education and support heterosexist institutions refused to provide. AIDS forced the heterosexual community to talk about homosexuality and begin to face their heterosexism, but before this happened, lesbians and gays took the steps necessary to set up education and support networks.

With limited finances and lack of organization, we set up networks that have lead the country in the fight against AIDS. The spirit of our community insures that we will survive.

The one I love most lay sleeping by me
*   under the same cover in the cool night,*
In the stillness in the autumn moonbeams
*   his face was inclined toward me,*
And his arm lay lightly around my breast
*   and that night I was happy.*

Walt Whitman
poet

Tender is the love we share. If people would stop and look at our love, really see our love, their hate might stop.

We grow up without images of the love men share between each other, without images of the love women share. The result: sometimes we're timid and even embarrassed about our love.

Nurture the love. Let others see your love. It's tender and beautiful to behold.

If Michelangelo were a heterosexual, the Sistine Chapel would have been painted basic white and with a roller.

Rita Mae Brown
writer

Historians have failed us. The contributions of lesbians and gays have been hidden. The underlying assumption in history books is that heterosexuals and only heterosexuals have made contributions to this world. Heterosexual and homosexual youths grow up without accurate historical facts. The only words spoken about lesbians and gays are the demeaning comments heard on the playground.

No wonder heterosexuals don't know anything about us. And, no wonder lesbians and gays grow up feeling shameful instead of proud.

Learn about our history. Claim our pride. As we share our history, we help re-educate the world.

*We are bound together by deeds of heroism,
by countless acts of political and social commitment.*

John D'Emilio
gay historian

We are family. We take care of our own. Yes,
we have disagreements just like all families do.
But when there is a need to reach out to our
lesbian and gay sisters and brothers, we readi-
ly do so. Just look at our heartfelt response to
the AIDS epidemic. Look at the way we provide support and friendships to our sisters and
brothers just coming out. A family of friends is
always waiting.

Rather than let the prejudice we face harm
us, we respond by coming together as family.
Nurture the family that supports and loves
you.

[About Alice B. Toklas]: *How prettily we swim. Not in water. Not on land. But in love.*

Gertrude Stein
writer

Our expressions of love have been denied and hidden for too long. Lesbians and gays are now reclaiming their history. We unabashedly celebrate the love and passion of previous generations of lesbians and gays. Their lives and loves are no longer hidden.

We no longer allow the world to deny our love. We share their stories out of love, to reclaim our past, as testimonies of a love that has always existed and always will.

So big a thing as the transformation of the world hinges on so small a thing as the transformation of the human heart.

Episcopal Bishop Browning

Transformation of the heart often occurs unknowingly in day-to-day acts of love and caring that might seem insignificant. A heart changes upon seeing a gay man care for his ill lover. A heart changes upon seeing lesbian and gay couples lovingly teaching their young children how to read. A heart changes upon hearing the struggles lesbians and gays face in their day-to-day lives.

Let others see the care and love you give. Our acts of love transform hearts.

When I see 600 individuals willingly subjecting themselves to arrest on the steps of the Supreme Court to protest its homophobia, then I am grateful to be gay because I belong to a people who have right on their side, and I know that justice is on the way.

Arnie Kantrowitz
writer

We are a courageous and proud community. Lesbians and gays are no longer willing to allow the injustices we face go unnoticed. Our anger is righteous. Because of our courage and pride we will persevere until we gain the respect and rights we, as all other people, deserve.

As part of the disenfranchised we are taught and forced to sit back. We no longer need to do so. And, as part of reclaiming our pride, we must not sit back.

It's okay to protest. It's okay to say you're angry. Speak up!

She say, Celie, tell the truth, have you ever found God in church? I never did. I just found a bunch of folks hoping for him to show. Any God I ever felt in church I brought in with me.

Alice Walker
writer

Many lesbians and gays have these exact sentiments. Experiences with traditional religious institutions often were shallow and lacking in meaning. The message was "God is outside of you" not "God is within you." We were also told "God doesn't come to homosexuals." Even Celie, a woman denied educational opportunities, was able to see beyond this nonsense.

Since we are all part of creation, each of us carries God within us (however we choose to define God). In spite of efforts to convince lesbians and gays they can't be spiritual, we intuitively know a spirit celebrates our gayness. Reclaim it, it's yours!

Now is the moment to reach out to someone. It's all up to you.

N. Swanston and T. Cox
songwriters

Sometimes it's hard to reach out for support. Most lesbians and gays grow up emotionally and physically isolated from "out" lesbians and gays and from supportive nongays. We have learned, on some inner level, that it's not safe to reach out. This pattern can carry over into adulthood. Even when we know we need and deserve support, we still hesitate in reaching out.

Take time today to reach out to someone. Building support is building family.

If I cannot air this pain and alter it, I will surely die of it.

Audre Lorde
writer

To survive, to live, we must release our pain. Growing up lesbian or gay is still painful. Are you hiding your pain as a means to hide being gay? Do you recognize the pain you have endured or have you buried it so deep that you have convinced yourself there is no pain to release?

Take time to examine the pain you have suffered. Write about it; talk about it; do something with it. If the pain is not released, the anger can turn to self-hatred and bitterness, or an inability to get close to others.

It's okay to share your pain. Releasing the pain is healing.

Gays sometimes lost their freedom because heterosexuals wanted to rob them of it, he thought, but sometimes gays lost their freedom because they were willing to give it away.

Randy Shilts
journalist/author

Freedom must be won over and over again. Lesbians and gays cannot be content with asking for freedom. We must demand basic civil rights other people already take for granted.

Individuals and groups who have been victimized learn to "settle for less than" as part of the victimization they endured. Settling for less than, even after we're out, is a continuation of the pattern of victimization we know too well.

Ask yourself if you still find yourself settling for less than you deserve. Are you giving away your freedom or fighting for it? Be a survivor: continue to demand what you deserve.

All you folks think you run my life
Say I should be willing to compromise
I say all you demons go back to hell
I'll save my soul save myself

Tracy Chapman
singer/songwriter

Have you ever thought that maybe you are letting other people run your life by hiding in the closet? It's easy to recognize the hiding we may be doing, but do you recognize how the hiding is giving other people control over your very own life?

Think of the control you're giving others when you hide your "gay books" before they come over, when you hide your lover's photo or when you maintain two bedrooms to "look straight" for all your straight friends. How out of control is your life? How many compromises have you made?

It's time to take back control of your own life. Healing involves taking back control because with it comes pride.

I believe more than ever that our greatest gains are made not through congressional or court decisions but rather by gay men and lesbians making the individual personal decision to come out.

Joe Steffan
U.S. Naval Academy graduate

It's true that with civil rights legislation more lesbians and gays will come out of the closet and reclaim their pride. However, if we're waiting for legislation to "prove we are okay," we're giving others too much power.

Our sense of pride needs to develop with or without legislation. We may *want* others approval but we do not *need* others approval to reclaim our pride.

We'll certainly continue to demand acceptance and respect. However, we are capable of affirming our pride with or without other's approval. Don't give others too much power. You have more power than you realize. Claim it and use it!

In the end, antiblack, antifemale, and all forms of discrimination are equivalent to the same thing . . . antihumanism.

Shirley Chisholm
politician

All forms of oppression are interrelated. The challenge is to simultaneously celebrate our sameness and our differentness.

Heterosexism will not be dismantled while racism, sexism and other forms of oppression exist. Just as we expect and demand that heterosexuals work through their prejudices toward lesbians and gays, we must not perpetuate any form of oppression within our own community. We have experienced the harmful effects. We must not perpetuate oppression.

Discover the diversity among ourselves! Celebrate it! This celebration helps all heal and keeps all safe.

I change myself, I change the world.

Gloria Anzaldua
writer

Each time I look inside and take pride in being gay I precipitate change in others. Others can no longer deny my existence. Others see my pride.

I do not reclaim my pride so that others may benefit, nonetheless others do benefit. And many join in my celebration of pride.

Once you have opened your arms to your Genuine Self you are free.

Sally Fisher
educator/writer
AIDS Mastery Workshop

We face many struggles in our process of self-acceptance. Initially, it can involve hiding our homosexuality out of fear of rejection and societal disapproval. Each time we conceal our homosexuality, however, our very being is wounded. Each time we hide, our shame stays trapped inside.

After hiding our homosexuality for long periods of time, we may be so adept at denying the pain that we say it doesn't exist.

Our process of healing involves breaking through this denial in order to release the shame. That means a continual process of being open about one's homosexuality.

Find new ways to be out as a means to release your shame.

The bitterest tears shed over graves are for words left unsaid and deeds left undone.

Harriet Beecher Stowe
writer

Cultural victimization initially results in the oppressed as accomplices in their own passivity. Hope is given up. Dreams are not realized. Life is without meaning.

How have you remained passive and denied yourself your dreams because you were taught to believe "good things don't come to homosexuals anyhow?"

Year upon year passes quickly. Remain an accomplice to the victimization you have already endured or overcome it. Take action on your dreams; not talk, rather action, action, action!

If Rosa Parks had taken a poll before she sat down in the bus in Montgomery, she'd still be standing.

Mary Frances Berry

Just do it! How often do we get bogged down thinking we better check it out with everyone else and make sure they're okay with our plan. One of the harmful effects of victimization is lack of self-confidence. Along with this lack of confidence is the tendency to put others' needs ahead of our own, making sure others are comfortable at considerable cost to ourselves.

It's time to stop trying to make sure everyone else is comfortable. What are your needs? For once, put yourself first.

The diagnosis of homosexuality as a "disorder" is a contributing factor to the pathology of those homosexuals who do become mentally ill . . . Nothing is more likely to make you sick than being constantly told that you are sick.

Ronald Gold
National Lesbian and Gay Task Force (NLGTF)

Shame is learned, not innate. The shame we struggle with stems from the fact that we have been abused by society, not that we are lesbian or gay. To tell young children that homosexuals are sick, sinful and perverted is a form of abuse. These hateful messages are the real pathology. It's not surprising for lesbian/gay children to reach adolescence struggling with self-hatred passed on from society. Heterosexual children also grow up filled with hateful messages of homophobia.

These hateful messages are learned and can be stopped. Gay and straight, we must work to end these messages. Hate harms everyone.

I am proud to be a gay man because of the gay men who have taught me truth and beauty: Homer, Socrates, Aristophanes, Horace, Martial, Aelred of Rivelaux, Hopkins and Auden.

John G.

When I initially asked John to think about reasons he was proud to be gay, he responded like many lesbians and gays: "Reasons to be proud? I'm not sure I can think of any." Two weeks later John presented me with an incredibly beautiful and powerful list of reasons why he was indeed proud to be a gay man, beginning with the statement above. John found that with some searching he was able to identify numerous reasons to be filled with pride.

Reclaiming our pride is part of our healing from cultural victimization. Don't let a heterosexist society keep you from celebrating your heritage. Discover the reasons to be proud of your community.

Each had his past shut in him like the leaves of a book known to him by heart; and his friends can only read the title.

Virginia Woolf
writer

The disparity between what we show to the world and what we hide inside can cause much pain. In the closet to some, out to others. Continual push and pull—and at what cost to ourselves?

We get to write the chapters of our lives. Write them the way you want to live them, and the way you want to be remembered.

Being powerful and at the same time empowering is a high state of consciousness and spirituality.

Rob Eichberg
writer and co-creator of
The Experience Weekend

Coming out is a spiritual process. Spirituality is tied to self-love. The coming out process, from denial to tolerance, acceptance and celebrating being lesbian and gay is possibly the most spiritual undertaking for each of us today. We must become deeply aware of who we are and experience the joy and pain of the paths we have traversed. We must examine how we currently live our lives, and determine whether we are taking good care of ourselves and our families. These are all parts of our spiritual journey.

Life is a spiritual journey only when we are true to ourselves.

To be "cured" against one's will and cured of states which we may not regard as disease is to be put on a level with those who have not yet reached the age of reason.

C. S. Lewis
writer

How many lesbians and gays have been sent to psychiatrists to "cure" them of their homosexuality? It's taken decades for the American Psychiatric Association to recognize the cruelty in such treatment and some still refuse to acknowledge it.

If you are one of those lesbians and gays sent to a therapist to be cured, remember that homosexuality is not the problem, hatred and bigotry are.

You can enter the age of reason even if others are still in the Dark Ages.

Gay people are especially empowered because we are able to identify with both sexes and can see into more than one world at once, having the capacity to see from more than one point of view at a time . . . One of the major homosexual/shamanic functions in any society is to cross over between the two essentially different worlds and reveal them to each other.

Judy Grahn
writer

Lesbians and gays as special people. Not something we've heard often in the 20th century. Yet in other cultures special people, shamans, have been homosexual. They're elevated in status because of the gift to see more than one world at a time.

The struggle of living in two worlds today is also a great teacher. Today, each of us has the opportunity to reframe our homosexuality as a gift.

We do not grow absolutely, chronologically. We grow sometimes in one dimension and not in another, unevenly . . . We are mature in one realm, childish in another.

Anaïs Nin
writer

Most lesbians and gays weren't allowed the opportunity to have the adolescence they deserved—an adolescence filled with guidance, nurturing, exploration and care for same sex relationships. We may come out at age 25 or 45. Chronologically we're an adult, but emotionally we're an adolescent.

Give yourself permission to experience this second adolescence, the adolescence you weren't allowed to have in your teenage years. At the same time, utilize the wisdom age brings to navigate the storms of adolescence. Find a nurturing way to explore new terrain.

That it will never come again
Is what makes life so sweet.

Emily Dickinson
poet

And "that it will never come again," is all the reason to make haste in being the lesbian or gay person you want to be.

Let go of the shame *now*. Stop the hiding *now*. Be yourself *now*. Your dreams, hopes and goals can be realized. It's up to you to make them happen.

Each one of us has the power to claim our own truth. And fully love and accept ourselves—right now!

The Living Earth Project
at the 1993 March on Washington

Heterosexuals have tried to convince us they have the market on "truth!" How can they claim our "truth" when they don't know us? When an individual or group in the majority or with more power tries to force their "truth" onto others, it's an abuse of power.

To gain our power back we must claim our own truth. We must accept ourselves for who we are. We must celebrate who we are and join in celebration with others for who they are. There is no other truth.

Our strength lies in our diversity.

slogan/sign
at the 1993 March on Washington

We were taught to place a superior value on all things white, male and heterosexual, to name a few. We have not been taught to value anything else. We have not been taught to value diversity. And, why not? The insecurity of those holding power often perpetuates their abuse of power.

Power is not maintained over the long run by limiting access to others. We are beginning to recognize that power ought to be shared.

It is not only that our strength lies in our diversity but our hope lies in celebrating our diversity.

When you finally come out, there's a pain that stops, and you know it will never hurt like that again, no matter how much you lose . . .

Paul Monette
writer

Are you comfortable in the closet? We may convince ourselves and actually believe we are, but how much of this so called "comfortability" is a result of unknowingly buying into the message, "It's okay to be gay. Just keep it quiet and out of sight"? Probably more than we realize because after breaking down the closet door we experience a breadth of life so freeing that we cannot believe we hesitated so long to come out.

The results of the victimization we suffer run deeper than we know. Comfort in the closet is believing that we will be accepted when silent.

Don't be fooled. Don't buy into the myths. There is no lasting comfort in the closet.

We're Here! We're Queer! Get Used To It.
Queer Nation chant

A new era of gay activism has arisen. The message for heterosexual America is bold and clear: Homosexuality is *not* the problem. Heterosexism and homophobia *are*!

This message is equally important for lesbians and gays. It is a reminder to each of us that when we recognize that homosexuality is *not* the problem, but bigotry and prejudice are, we take a step further in our healing. We move from victim to survivor. And when we can proclaim "Get used to it," we don't just survive, we thrive!

Move the weight from your shoulders. Place it where it belongs. Let the healing continue.

We can learn to work and to speak when we are afraid in the same way we have learned to work and speak when we are tired. For we have been socialized to respect fear more than our own needs for language and definition, and while we wait in silence for that final luxury of fearlessness, the weight of that silence will choke us . . .

Audre Lorde
writer

How many times have we thought about coming out, holding our partner's hand in public, reading a gay newspaper on the subway, but our own fear is greater than the risk at hand? Or the number of times we've put ourselves through emotional gymnastics about coming out to someone and their response was simply, "No big deal," or "That's great." Then we say to ourselves, "What have I been so afraid of?" Unleash your fear! The next step is likely to be easier than you realize.

Androgyny suggests a spirit of reconciliation between the sexes.

Carolyn Heilbrun

The struggle to accept homosexuality is tied to gender role stereotypes. Oppression of lesbians and gays is interrelated with devaluing women. Those things viewed as male are considered more valuable, while all things female are devalued.

The androgyny of many lesbians and gays places us at the forefront of challenging these rigid stereotypes. Acceptance of homosexuality means a greater understanding and balance between the sexes. Androgyny on the other hand, suggests that each of us embrace both the feminine and masculine within ourselves.

When I stand weeping in a field surrounded by a memorial patchwork of quilt panels lovingly made to commemorate our friends whom AIDS has taken, and when I see that it requires acres of ground to tell of a sorrow eloquent in its silence, then I am grateful to be gay because I belong to a people who can create beauty even in the face of death.

Arnie Kantrowitz
writer

We are creative. We are compassionate. Our love will know no end.

Consider the risks lesbians and gays take. Consider the struggles we face. Have you reminded yourself that we are truly a courageous and caring people? Have you utilized your creative talents?

The therapist said, "If you get married, your feelings for women will go away." So I got married. I was married one year when I fell in love with a woman. I had never experienced any kind of feeling like that ever. Not with no guy. I knew those feelings were never going away.

Joyce Hunter
co-founder
Harvey Milk High School
for Lesbian and Gay Teens

The pressures to conform to heterosexuality are tremendous. Therapists, who should be helping us heal from the prejudice and victimization we face, sometimes participate in continuing to mislead us.

Intuitively, we know where our attraction lies. To deny our attraction is to deny who we really are.

The sooner we acknowledge and accept our attractions, the sooner our healing begins.

A peacefulness follows any decision, even the wrong one.

Rita Mae Brown
writer

Lesbians and gays agonize over coming out to others. The emotional gymnastics we put ourselves through while trying to guess how others will handle our coming out is exhausting! We can't predict. Still we must act.

Before we speak out, the stress builds. The coming out, regardless of the response, releases the tension of maintaining the secret. Coming out reclaims some inner peace; and with this inner peace, it becomes less important how others handled the coming out.

We are the experts on ourselves.

Frank Kameny
founder
Mattachine Society of Washington, D.C.

People who know nothing about lesbians and gays have been trying to define us for decades. There is a grave discrepancy between "history about us" versus "history by us."

We reclaim our power each time we loudly reject others' definitions and instead define ourselves. Our history and experience must be described from our perspective.

Challenge the misguided perceptions about you by defining yourself and your experiences.

God is inside you and inside everybody else.
You came into the world with God. But only
them that search for it inside find it.

Alice Walker
writer

Spirituality is neither given to us nor taken
away from us. Religious zealots that identify
"the saved" from "the lost," in essence, are
telling us how they draw their lines of bigotry.
Their foolery unraveled, lesbians and gays
reclaim our spirituality, in part because of the
very prejudice we face.

We fearlessly search inward, propelling us
to a deeper spirituality.

Even after you come to terms with your homosexuality, you still carry those wounds from childhood that made you feel inferior, that make you feel you were not as good as the heterosexual male.

Barry Sandler
screenwriter

Childhood wounds are devastating. The disparaging and hateful "sissy," "dyke" and "fag" comments are painful and deeply embedded. Because these shaming messages become so entrenched in our being, we often-times grow up mistakenly believing our sense of inferiority is because of our homosexuality. Our struggles with feeling inferior are *not* because we're gay, but because we've been shamed repeatedly since childhood.

Don't blame yourself! Part of our healing is first to recognize that our struggles with inferiority are *not* because of who we are, but because of what has been done to us.

"Don't ask. Don't tell.
Bill Clinton, go to hell."

> protest following President Clinton's
> failure to end the ban
> on gays in the military

Change comes slowly for many. Bigotry takes different disguises. For years we heard "homosexuality is abnormal." More recently we've heard "it's okay to be gay, but keep it hidden." Unfortunately, the bigotry remains clear.

We don't ask heterosexuals to hide their heterosexuality. In all fairness how can we ask homosexuals to do so?

"Don't ask, don't tell?" It's a new "we're here, we're queer, get used to it world." Denial can only last so long.

A lesbian who consents to guilt for her sexual preference is her own worst oppressor. She accepts and internalizes prejudices and uses them against herself.

Sidney Abbott and Barbara Love
authors

We're taught to feel guilty and shameful about our homosexuality. We must recognize how we have been shamed before we can reclaim pride.

Growing up, what myths and negative stereotypes did you hear about homosexuality? Are you still buying into these myths?

Release the myths. Embrace the truth. Release the shame instilled by others. Embrace yourself.

That homosexuality has been a natural condition of kings, composers, engineers, poets, housewives and bus drivers, and that it has contributed more than its share of beauty and laughter to an ugly and ungrateful world should be obvious to anyone who is willing to peer beneath the surface.

Martin Greif
writer

A growing segment of society is willing to peer beneath the surface and acknowledge the contributions made by lesbians and gays. Because society has tried for so long to hide our contributions, we frequently grow up not knowing there are reasons to be proud of being lesbian or gay. Why are you proud?

If you struggle answering this question you too must peer beneath the surface to discover what lesbians and gays have done to make this a brighter world. The reasons are endless. Find them. Celebrate them.

When he scanned the smiling faces in the crowded bar, what he saw were not the furtive and frightened expressions of a haunted minority but a group of successful and well-adjusted people having a good time. This is paradise . . .

Randy Shilts
journalist/author

Upon coming out, many gays flock to gay bars. For years, gay bars were the *only* social outlet. Think back to the first time you found a group of lesbians and gays. Remember that sense of finally "coming home?" This is only the beginning, the awakening. To not move beyond these initial contacts with other lesbians and gays is like a child hanging on to Mom or Dad.

Each of us must find and create our own family. Our community is large and diverse. Don't limit your search for the loving and caring family you deserve. You are responsible for creating the best family you can.

OCTOBER 6

I'm a little tired of people feeling like they have a right to hate. Hate is hate.

Robert Byrd
TV producer

People continue to try to justify their hatred of lesbians and gays. Enough is enough. Individuals claim they are okay with homosexuality but are opposed to "special rights" for lesbians and gays. Their opposition of special rights is really a way to justify their hatred.

We must expose the hatred for what it is. Reach out for support so others' hatred doesn't prevent you from being yourself.

I am enjoying to the full that period of reflection which is the happiest conclusion to a life of action.

Willa Cather
author

In years to come, how will each of us reflect on our lives as lesbians and gays? Will we reflect on a life of action or a life of silence? Will we look back with fond memories? Will the pain still hurt us?

Hopefully, we will look back and see that even with the struggles we faced as lesbians and gays, we met the challenges and lived our lives fully. To delay being the person you want to be is to face a life of regret.

Today, take one action to be the lesbian or gay person you want to be.

I was fearful, but I realized that if I didn't conquer that fear, I just couldn't function. I decided I had to speak, that I'd have to take my chances, because it's better than to be afraid.

Paulette Goodman
past president
Federation of Parents and Friends
of Lesbians and Gays (PFLAG)

Our parents have a parallel coming out process. Once we come out to them, they begin their own coming out as parents of a lesbian or gay individual. They move from silence to tolerance, to acceptance and then to pride.

Some parents stay stuck in silence just as some lesbians and gays do. Parents are less likely to voice their pride when we stay stuck.

Show your pride. Express your pride. You'll help your parents in their coming out.

I think part of why I went on "Oprah" was revenge—not so much at my parents, but at that town. For picking on me, for making fun of me, for making my life miserable. For teaching me that gay was wrong, that I couldn't live my life. I bought into it for years and years and years. I shut down my life. I didn't live my life or share it. But I sure showed them.

Greg Brock
journalist

We take back our power and reclaim our lives when we find healthy ways to direct our anger at those people who caused us harm. And once we express this anger to those individuals, the ugly side of the anger we have buried inside begins to subside. We no longer walk in the shadow. We now walk in the light.

Regain power. Come out to others and say, "I'm gay and proud, and happy with my life in spite of all the hateful things done to me."

*Everybody knows if you are too careful you
are so occupied in being careful that you are
sure to stumble over something.*

Gertrude Stein
author

All those careful ways we tried to hide our
homosexuality only to find later that "everybody knew anyway!" We were so careful in
calling our lovers "roommates"; so careful in
hiding books and magazines when Mom and
Dad came to visit.

Eventually people discover, or we ultimately tell them, we're gay. But look at the time and
energy wasted on our part. These attempts to
mask our lives take a significant toll on us.

Lighten up. Loosen up. Be yourself.

When I see young men and old women come out of their closets and face being called faggots and dykes and pariahs and betrayers of the family dream, then I am honored to be gay because I belong to a people who are proud.

Arnie Kantrowitz
writer

Pride is the key that makes coming out possible. Where is your pride? Has it been buried in the avalanche of shaming messages about homosexuality? Has it sometimes seemed like you have little or no self-pride? If so, it's time to rediscover your pride.

Get involved with other lesbians and gays who can help you reclaim your pride. One individual with pride can spark change in others. Pride fuels coming out. Coming out further kindles your pride.

What we are is a crime, if it is a crime to love, For the god who made me live made me love.

Baudri of Bourgueil
Benedictine abbot/poet

To be able to express our love is a sign of health. Love is natural and enriching. To deny the love we have for our lesbian and gay sisters and brothers is to deny our own existence.

Current religious and state proceedings may see the love between two men and the love between two women as criminal, but often the rules, laws, etc., take a long time to catch up to understanding and reason. For example, it took the Catholic Church over 300 years to acknowledge that maybe they were wrong in calling Galileo a heretic for suggesting the Earth was round.

We know our love is real and true. The longer it takes for others to recognize this, the more foolish they look.

To be gay is to be overwhelmed with the attitudes of other people, and in order to free ourselves from that we have to put those aside and develop our own sense of what is right.

Harry Britt
politician

Growing up in a society where everyone is blindly assumed to be heterosexual, those of us who are homosexual must discard all the socialization to make us into something that we are not. Finding the "real me" can be difficult after being forced into roles that don't fit, combined with the lack of positive images of lesbians and gays.

Growth and maturity come with abandoning those false roles we have acquired under pressure, and asking ourselves some very essential questions: What are my interests? My personal needs? Am I living the life I want or a version of someone else's plan for me?

OCTOBER 14

When one is pretending, the entire body revolts.

Anaïs Nin
writer

We're certainly gaining a better understanding of the mind-body connection. People who have been victimized tend to have all sorts of physical or somatic complaints. Victimization, such as heterosexism and homophobia, contribute to self-hate and shame.

Our bodies, as temples, cannot stay physically healthy when we're filled with self-hate. Think of those days when you've struggled with feeling good about yourself and the stress has resulted in headaches, missed work or depression.

Healing emotionally contributes to physical well-being. And healing emotionally can only be complete when we stop the heterosexual masquerade.

What you will do matters. All you need is to do it.

Judy Grahn
writer

When over one million lesbians and gays gathered in Washington, D.C. for the 1993 March on Washington for Lesbian, Gay & Bi Equal Rights and Liberation, we told America we matter; that even though some people continue to deny our existence we are here, we are strong, we are becoming more visible and we will not go away.

For countless numbers of lesbians and gays the power in participating in the march came from the sense of community shared by over one million lesbians and gays brought together for a common purpose. For some it was the first time feeling in the majority. T-shirts galore expressed this pride and affirmation.

The challenge is to continue to express that pride. It matters even more once we return home. Wearing that T-shirt from the march at home makes a statement. It matters. Do it!

OCTOBER 16

The revolution begins at home.

Cherrie Moraga and Gloria Anzaldua
writers

Calls for justice and calls for equality do not begin in the streets. Calls for freedom grow from the years of pain held inside by countless lesbians and gays who have been demeaned, abused and forced into second class citizenship. Eventually the pain grows intolerable.

We must act. Simply demanding justice and reclaiming our pride become revolutionary acts.

Free our bodies. Free our minds. Free our hearts.

Tracy Chapman
singer/songwriter

Remnants of Victorian sexual attitudes pervade Western society. We live in a "sex-negative society"—restrictive attitudes abound that frown on knowing our sexual selves. On the other hand, sexual exploitation abounds, which is fueled by these rigid sexual stereotypes.

Our sexuality can be an affirming and celebratory part of our lives, rather than something that instills fear and shame. Release the fear. Release the shame. Integrate your sexuality into the whole of your life.

No, Mama, I wasn't "recruited." No seasoned homosexual ever served as my mentor. But you know what? . . . I wish someone older than me and wiser than the people in Orlando had taken me aside and said, "You're all right, kid. You can grow up to be a doctor or a teacher just like anyone else. You're not crazy or sick or evil . . . Most of all, though, you can love and be loved, without hating yourself for it."

Armistead Maupin
author

The misinformed and prejudiced continue to think that homosexuals are recruited as children and then become recruiters. To waste time and energy on such a silly prospect can be disheartening when so many lesbian and gay children are desperate for positive role models. Attempts to keep homosexuality hidden from these children is misuse of power and a form of sexual and emotional abuse. Children need to learn to value themselves. Be a role model.

The last refuge of intolerance is in not tolerating the intolerant.

George Eliot
writer

Lesbians and gays have typically been on the defense—defending ourselves from heterosexual prejudice that attempts to perpetuate harmful stereotypes.

We've done our part in dispelling these myths. It's time to take the offensive. It's time to take "the burden of proof" off of our shoulders. It's time to let the prejudiced know they are the ones that need to change, not us!

There's nothing I need from anyone except love and respect, and if anyone cannot give me those two things they have no place in my life.

Harvey Fierstein
actor/playwright

Don't settle for less than love and respect. Instilled with shame at an early age about our homosexuality from misinformed segments of society, we may reach adulthood finding ourselves tolerating all sorts of negative comments and actions. We grew up hearing we were "not okay" for being gay, and we tolerate behavior from others that reinforces "I'm not okay."

Growing up expecting negatives, we may not even recognize them for what they are: abuse! It's important to stop taking that kind of abuse from others.

You deserve love and respect. Don't tolerate anything less. Remember: We get to choose who we call family.

[interrupting the 1971 meeting of the American Psychiatric Association]: *Psychiatry is the enemy incarnate! . . . Psychiatry has waged a relentless war of extermination against us . . . you may take this as a declaration of war against you.*

Frank Kameny
founder
Mattachine Society of Washington, D.C.

For decades lesbians and gays have suffered the abuses of countless psychiatrists, psychologists and other so called "helping professionals" in their attempts to "cure" our homosexuality. We didn't need a cure. We don't want a cure. We only want homophobic and heterosexist individuals to leave us alone and let us define our own reality and experiences. Psychiatrists only faced their outdated beliefs when confronted by courageous gay individuals like Frank Kameny. Trust your intuition. Do not let "helping professionals" redefine what you know to be true.

I'd been living a lie, not being myself, not being open, carrying this tremendous burden around: It was a burden lifted, and now it was their's.

Gary Brock
journalist

In the 1950s the prevailing societal view was homosexuality is a problem. The burden was clearly on homosexuals.

In the 1970s, society began to hear about "homophobia." The focus changed to confronting heterosexuals about their prejudices and irrational fears of homosexuals.

In the 1990s lesbians and gays proudly proclaim "if you're still buying into all those myths about lesbians and gays, that's your problem, not mine." The burden has been lifted off our shoulders and heterosexuals now carry the burden of eradicating their own heterosexism.

Homosexuality is no longer the problem; heterosexism is.

We are strong, we are proud, and we are here to seek justice. We are here for our rights and our liberation . . . Look around you. Everyone here is an American Hero.

official program guide
at the 1993 National March on Washington

Lesbians and gays who are out are heroes because we say we are not going back in the closet in spite of continuing efforts to silence us. Our visibility is our power, not only because it educates others, but because visibility increases our own pride and self-respect.

A hero's power cannot be dismantled because it is based on personal pride.

In itself, homosexuality is as limiting as heterosexuality: the ideal should be to be capable of loving a woman or a man; either, a human being, without feeling fear, restraint or obligation.

Simone De Beauvoir
writer

It is remarkable that anyone has the capacity to love when our society tries to dictate who we love and how we love. Consider the harmful effects of sexism. Boys reach adulthood unable to show affection, care and love. Add to that the negative effects of heterosexism. We're taught disdain for attractions to members of the same sex. No wonder so many individuals reach adulthood not knowing how to form and maintain caring relationships. This contributes to self-hate and anger displaced toward others.

Lesbian and gay people are challenging the world to look at the silly proscriptions surrounding who we love. Love knows no rules.

The courts and Congress are simply a reflection of society. By coming out to our friends, families, and co-workers, we can help change society from the inside out. Only then will we win the lasting political and legal gains we seek.

Joe Steffan
U.S. Naval Academy graduate

Occasionally, politicians have a vision of a better world and take action, regardless of how unpopular. More often they simply respond to changing societal norms. History continues to teach us that when it comes to basic civil liberties, legislators often don't protect and safeguard all individuals.

This is why lesbians and gays are forced to demand their rights. As individuals, it's important that we raise our voices and demand equal treatment. Each time we do so, we heal from the years of prejudice. Each time we do so, we take a step in reclaiming our pride. We'll persist until society catches up.

....

My way of coping was to be an overachiever and to give my parents something to be proud of.

Deborah L. Johnson
along with Zandra Rolon sued a
Los Angeles restaurant for refusing to
serve them as a couple and won their case

Many lesbians and gays struggle with issues of perfectionism . . . overcompensating for our low self-esteem by trying to be perfect. If we are "perfect" and then someone finds out we're gay, maybe we'll still be "okay" in their eyes. But if we start out "just okay," maybe they will completely reject us once we do come out. The drive to prove ourselves is often based on these irrational beliefs.

We give others tremendous power when we let them decide whether or not "we're okay." Stopping the approval-seeking by validating ourselves is another step in our healing.

The simple, obvious thing would have been to go to the senior prom with a girl . . .

Aaron Fricke

Too frequently, doing the simple and the obvious gets translated into doing what others expect but what is unnatural for ourselves. How strange that the simple and obvious is not the natural?

Healing from heterosexism involves making the natural simple and obvious once again. How natural it is to hold the hand of the one you love and walk down the street, or to kiss your partner good-bye at the airport. These are simple actions. These are natural actions. But after years of parents, teachers and clergy telling us they are unnatural, we question them.

What is natural comes from the heart. It is simple, obvious and beautiful to behold. Free the natural inside yourself. As you do, the choices become obvious and you are able to reach a greater peace, free from the encumbrances of others' unnatural expectations.

Some of the people who hate us think we're out to indoctrinate their children. Frankly, we're trying to save their children from suicide.

Paul Monette
author

Heterosexism is based on the false assumption that all children are born heterosexual. When a child is born, most people do not even entertain the possibility that the child may be lesbian or gay. What a surprise to later find that one's daughter or son is homosexual. How ironic to assume they would automatically be heterosexual and then to condemn lesbians and gays for indoctrinating their children when the children are already lesbian and gay.

We can help our parents break through this myth so future parents will not automatically assume all their children will be straight.

I am proud to be a gay man because it has helped me to work for the freedom of women, people of color, citizens of the Third World and all who are oppressed by those who choose to maintain their power and security at all costs.

John G.

The reluctance to accept homosexuality is about maintaining power. Power and control are based on selfishness, insecurity and fear of those different than ourselves. When we are comfortable with ourselves, we realize there is no need to fear and compete with others. When we celebrate both our differences and similarities, we are better able to share with, rather than oppress, those who are different.

Lesbians and gays have been and continue to be oppressed. We can learn from oppression and help others understand that all individuals deserve and need to be respected.

Healing means eliminating not only heterosexism, but racism, sexism, classism and all other "isms."

When rights are not acknowledged they must be fought for and won. When liberty is denied, it must be demanded. We do not ask for lesbian and gay power, it already exists. It lives in our wisdom, our vigilance, and our righteous anger.

official program guide
at the 1993 March on Washington

Our power lies in our resolve to continue to fight the injustices we face. We realize that with our advances we will also suffer setbacks. Our work will take much time. Yet, we persist because we are firm in our commitment to be treated fairly and with respect.

Those who continue to oppress us fail to realize that their attempts only bolster our vigilance and fuel our anger. Though the struggle is long and difficult, remember to take pride in our vigilance and persistence in securing justice.

I have never come across anyone in whom the moral sense was dominant who was not heartless, cruel, vindictive, log-stupid and entirely lacking in the smallest sense of humanity.

Oscar Wilde
writer

Why is it that those people who claim to have a monopoly on morality are the same people teaching hatred and bigotry? Morality is not about adhering to a rigid set of beliefs to maintain one's power while simultaneously subordinating others that do not adhere to the rigid beliefs. Morality is about expressing the kindness, caring, nurturing and loving within each of us. Morality ought to draw us together, not separate.

While the "moral zealots" focus on divisiveness, let's focus on what draws us together.

There's promise in a quilt. It's not a shroud or a tombstone. It's so important for people whose greatest enemy is despair. The worst thing that could happen to us is to despair and to stop living and loving and fighting.

Cleve Jones
founder
Names Project

Have you lost some of your hope or given up even one of your dreams? Individuals who regularly face prejudice and discrimination often do not realize the victimization they have suffered causes loss of hope and dreams.

Frequently we set our standards low or just miss success. We don't complete our degree or go for the job promotion because we have internalized the message that "lesbians and gays are never successful or happy." Giving in to the victimization is the greatest despair. It robs us of our hope and we don't even realize it.

Keep living. Keep loving. Keep fighting.

When everyone's sharing their hope
Then love will win through.

N. Swanston and T. Cox
songwriters

At times it may seem that it is not possible to be the lesbian or gay individual you want to be . . . living your life exactly as you choose. But there is always hope because it is always possible.

Keep your hopes and dreams alive by sharing them with supportive others. Isolation can kill dreams. Sharing with others increases validation and strength. It keeps hope alive and supports us in making the changes we dream of.

Cruelty is the only sin.

Ellen Glasgow

We grow up hearing "homosexuality is a sin." Homosexuality is not a sin, the cruelty we face is. Consider the tauntings we faced as children on school playgrounds that teachers let go unnoticed. Consider the "fag" jokes we hear at work that supervisors do not confront. Consider the messages of hate we still hear from some religious leaders.

The message that "homosexuality is sin" results in many lesbians and gays reaching adolescence feeling shameful about their very being.

Release the shame by recognizing the hatred and cruelty as the true sins.

[On his diocese becoming the first to publicly support blessing lesbian and gay relationships.]: *I find it difficult to believe that a church that blesses dogs in a Virginia fox hunt can't find a way to bless life-giving, lasting relationships between human beings.*

John Spong
Episcopal bishop

We already validate our relationships in holy unions, marriage ceremonies and celebrations. We will continue to do so with and without the support of traditional religious institutions. However, there is hope in the knowledge that some leaders in traditional religious institutions see the hypocrisy of the way lesbians and gays are treated and speak up, even in the face of church censure.

The important element is that visible, public forms of acknowledging our relationships increase their credibility. Our celebrations are a way to affirm our relationships on a personal level while simultaneously telling others that our relationships are valid!

The only place you can ever expect to feel whole is within yourself.

Sally Fisher
educator/writer
AIDS Mastery Workshop

We may initially view coming out with pain and trepidation. However, it is a deep occasion of the spirit. Coming out is about healing from cultural prejudice.

Our journey to heal is a spiritual journey because it is the process of reclaiming our being and becoming "whole." Wholeness and spirituality are interrelated.

After the fear and pain of coming out dissipate, take time to reflect on your continuing coming out process as a spiritual journey. There are many paths for healing and reclaiming pride as there are many spiritual journeys.

Cultural prejudice had not only succeeded in making most heterosexuals hate gays; it had succeeded in making most gay people hate themselves.

Randy Shilts
journalist/author

Lesbians and gays need one vital message as they begin acknowledging and accepting their homosexuality: Lesbians and gays do not hate themselves because they are gay. They learn to hate themselves because of heterosexism and homophobia. Cultural prejudice convinces many gays that self-hatred is "part of being homosexual." Wrong! Homosexuality doesn't cause self-hatred. Self-hatred is bred out of shaming cultural messages.

The process of healing from cultural prejudice involves taking the burden off of your shoulders and placing it where it belongs. This is not about you being a "bad" person because you're gay. This is about recognizing how society has treated you unfairly and moving on.

There is often in people to whom "the worst" had happened an almost transcendent freedom, for they have faced "the worst" and survived it.

Carol Pearson

Coming out as lesbian or gay is a lifelong process. Initially, it may seem abhorrent because of our own fears, rejection by others and unresolved internalized myths about homosexuality. If we can find support from others more enlightened than ourselves and if the forces of cultural prejudice are not too embedded in our minds and bodies, coming out will be transformed into a healing process and spiritual journey.

We learn that cultural prejudice no longer needs to harm us. We reclaim our identities as lesbian and gay and create a personal journey, not a journey pandered to heterosexist prejudice. Our journey is transcendent. Our journey is freedom. Our journey is a spiritual journey.

[Title of autobiography]: *The Lord is My Shepherd and He Knows I'm Gay.*

Reverend Troy Perry
founder
Metropolitan Community Church

Reclaiming our spirituality is part of healing from heterosexism. We may remain tied to the religious traditions we grew up with or we may reject them because they reject us. Some of us continue with traditional religious institutions because we're not about to let others "play God" and say who can and can't worship. For others, institutions must be rejected because their bigotry causes too much pain.

Out of frustration and anger we may give up on our spirituality. Remember, for some persons religion helps access spirituality whereas for others religion gets in the way. There are many paths to reclaiming our spirituality. After being told that lesbians and gays cannot be spiritual, we now know we have the ability to choose our own path.

For me there's no closet to go back to. I don't have a thing to do with closets. I don't even see how you have the option to run back in once you run out and deal, and I prefer it out so much more.

Essex Hemphill
poet

Accepting our own homosexuality may begin with bouncing in and out of the closet. It's a reminder of the detrimental effects of growing up in a heterosexist society. It may be an "on again/off again" process of releasing all the shaming messages we grew up with. But once we've acknowledged our own homosexuality, we may still participate in "out of the closet to some and in the closet to others."

Full self-acceptance does not occur when this game continues. How can it when we're denying who we are to a substantial number of people in our world?

You've opened that closet door and stepped out. It's time to shut it behind you.

Whereas heteros believe that spirituality requires the denial of carnality . . . our early sexual and sensual discoveries constitute for us the gateway to the growth of spirit in heart and mind.

Harry Hay
gay activist

The path to spirituality involves reclaiming our sexuality. If spirituality involves a deep understanding of ourselves and our interconnections with others, how can this be fostered if we deny our homosexuality or are not yet celebrating our homosexuality?

Lesbians and gays who have not yet reclaimed their pride about their homosexuality remain at the beginning of their spiritual journey. To let our spirituality flourish we must embrace our homosexuality because it is an integral part of who we are.

Find fulfilling ways to celebrate your homosexuality. It's part of your spiritual journey.

There's a glorious, ecstatic feeling in being seen, in being out there, especially after so many years of hiding. This is me, come and take it.

Sara Cytron
comedian

Think back to that glow you had as a child, that youthful spontaneity and energy that was so apparent before the shaming messages began to take their toll. Then, after years of hearing "it's not okay to be gay" we reach adulthood without that personal glow that tells the world we're vibrant and full of life. The shaming messages zapped away our zest for life.

Coming out restores that zest. Being out and open refuels the glow we lost during our childhood. There is no clearer indicator of that glow than when we are out, open and proud.

Don't settle for just living life. *Celebrate* your life.

*I know that you cannot live on hope alone.
But without it, life is not worth living.*

Harvey Milk
former San Francisco city supervisor

As children we're taught that to be gay is to be a failure. As the stereotype goes, homosexuality breeds contempt and self-loathing. But it is *not* homosexuality that breeds self-hatred. It is shaming stereotypes that perpetuate and instill self-hatred.

To recognize that our self-esteem is not tied to our inherent homosexuality, but to how we're treated as lesbians and gays is a necessary step in our coming out. We stop blaming our homosexuality for our struggles, and instead recognize the power of the shaming messages we have endured. Then we can let go of the shaming messages and begin to reclaim our personal power—that which was lost as a result of the shaming messages we grew up with.

There were closets within the closet, and a lingering self-hatred that even the joy of connection couldn't solve. What love gives you is the courage to face the secrets you've kept from yourself, a reason to open the rest of the doors.

Paul Monette
writer

Coming out is not a one-time event, but a lifelong process. After self-recognition and acknowledgment that we are gay, the process of coming out to others follows. But coming out goes much beyond the "telling" of our homosexuality: it involves dismantling the facades we presented for years. It's no longer acting or thinking the way others would prefer. It's about discovering ourselves.

When we feel the freedom to look inside and unabashedly say "this is me," we engage in a remarkable journey. A journey that then allows us to be intimate with others. Coming out is discovery, and is necessary for true intimacy. Coming out is living and loving.

One doesn't realize how inundated we are by heterosexuality until one experiences images from an alternate reality.

Chris Paros and Brenda Griffin
from a letter in *Out* magazine

Young children are told over and over that there's only one way to be, and that is heterosexual. Of course lesbian and gay children grow up feeling like there is something wrong with them because they know they're not heterosexual. We are forced to view the world from a "heterosexual" perspective. The result is that even we may not expect images of lesbians and gays in the media.

Part of our coming out process is shifting our perspective from a "heterosexual" to "homosexual" view of the world. It's like taking off a pair of eyeglasses that provided a distorted view. As you begin to focus more clearly, you will not be sidetracked by attempts to distort reality.

I want to break down people's stereotypes about lesbians. No one knows what a lesbian is anyway. We're all different.

Janis Ian
singer/songwriter

Lesbians and gays grow up hearing how they are "different." Different meaning something negative. As children we do not experience our awakening sexuality as negative until others label it as negative. Our sexual orientation is different from heterosexuals, but it is not negative. Special is a better word. Recognizing differences as "special" forces a re-examination of what we were taught as children. To live together and respect others, our focus must switch to valuing differences.

As you feel more comfortable about yourself, the differences you see in others will not be threatening to your self-esteem, but will instead build bridges to others.

It was necessary to break out of the silence. For lo these many years I had been resisting who I am. To exclude my gayness was a denial of God—and I think I can say that it was a blasphemous act.

E. Otis Charles
Episcopal bishop

Denying our homosexuality is denying our spirituality. To develop our spirituality we must be true to ourselves and acknowledge and accept our homosexuality. Our spirituality is tied to our level of self-acceptance. How can we foster our spirituality if we hold on to remnants of self-hate?

Spirituality involves loving ourselves so that we can reach out to others. Spirituality then, is how we live our lives . . . nurturing, loving and caring for ourselves and others.

If you do not tell the truth about yourself you cannot tell it about other people.

Virginia Woolf
writer

Focus on your own journey. This is difficult after years in the closet. We are forced to view our behavior from others' perspective when we are in the closet. How will they interpret what I say? What will they say about my actions?

To focus on our own journey we must learn to stop this preoccupation with what others may think. Instead, we focus on interpreting the world from our very own perspective. I get to choose my actions and express my ideas in my own way.

Filtering the world from a heterosexual perspective keeps you from knowing yourself. After years of letting others charter your course, you now can choose to focus on your own journey.

Standing with his nose pressed against the cold windowpane of heterosexuality, the outsider imagines that everything on the other side of the glass is peaceful, permanent, cozy. I have terrible news for him: Inside, they're longing to get out.

Quentin Crisp
author

Our society deifies heterosexuality while it simultaneously vilifies homosexuality. Children grow up believing that to be successful is to be heterosexual, married and have children. Even lesbians and gays learn to praise all things heterosexual. Our quest for freedom is not to mimic a "normal, heterosexual lifestyle." The lesbian and gay community challenges all people to take this narrow perspective of heterosexuality from its pedestal and instead to celebrate the richness of the variety of heterosexual and homosexual lifestyles.

Don't follow in mere footsteps. Create the life you desire.

The only thing keeping me from kissing my lover in public is . . . me.

Rex Wockner
writer

How many times have you avoided public displays of affection with someone of the same sex when there was no real danger present? Why would we avoid a hug when meeting a friend on the street? Why would we refrain from kissing our partners "so long" at the airport?

Frequently this is not about a real danger to ourselves, but instead an example of our lingering shame due to heterosexism. Our restraint in these situations perpetuates our victimization. If it's not natural for us, how could others see it as natural and normal?

Don't be your own worst enemy. Be yourself.

When you make a world tolerable for yourself, you make a world tolerable for others.

Anaïs Nin
writer

When we come out to ourselves, the ramifications are threefold. It is the first step in self-love as we heal from the negative effects of heterosexism.

Second, as we grow to celebrate our gayness, other lesbians and gays still struggling with self-acceptance will take note and find strength in our actions.

Finally, our coming out challenges heterosexuals to re-examine all the stereotypes they learned about lesbians and gays.

Self-love generates tolerance. Love yourself, and the effects of your love will reach out to others.

Of course it is extremely difficult to like oneself in a culture which thinks you are a disease.

Chrystos

To teach children lies and to teach children to hate themselves is the worst abuse lesbians and gays have endured. No wonder so many lesbians and gays struggle with self-acceptance. And then, society teaches us to believe that self-hate is a result of homosexuality.

Our struggles with self-acceptance are not because we're gay, but because we've been abused. Recognizing this as abuse is the first step in healing. By naming the abuse we are able to move forward and reclaim our pride.

She had started people talking about gay rights. The love that dare not speak its name had become the love that would not shut up.

Randy Shilts
journalist/author

Victor Hugo once wrote "All the forces in the world are not so powerful as an idea whose time has come." Lesbian and gay visibility is here to stay, and over time legal systems will reflect this reality. It's difficult to pick up a newspaper today without some coverage about lesbians and gays. Of course, these articles are not always accurate or positive, but even the least poignant article is a continual reminder that lesbians and gays are not going back in the closet.

This is an opportunity for those struggling with coming out to do so. The climate is right now! For those of us who are out, continue to proclaim your pride. It provides strength and hope for those still struggling.

You [gays and lesbians] are the nobility of our time . . . History will show the homophobes as despicable . . .

Mathilde Krim
co-founder
American Foundation for AIDS Research

As we advocate for acceptance and respect we must remind ourselves of our courage. We must take pride in our efforts to fight injustice. It is easy to lose sight of how remarkable we are when our efforts only bring piecemeal changes. Noble efforts are not based on immediate gains. Noble efforts are humanitarian efforts. They are based on strong convictions of justice; our generation may not fully see this justice, but hopefully it will be seen by the next generation.

History will recognize our efforts as noble and our community as courageous.

For years I ate Thanksgiving dinner with my family and couldn't speak of my friends. Then for years I rejected my family and celebrated the holidays with my friends. Now I can mix and match as I wish. And I am grateful to be gay because I belong to a people who have come very far very quickly and who are destined to go farther still.

Arnie Kantrowitz
writer

Coming out is a lifelong process. Initially, we come out to ourselves. Next, we begin to share our homosexuality with others. We might immerse ourselves in the lesbian and gay community, excluding heterosexuals, in order to gain support, reclaim our pride and find safety in community and family.

However, coming out does not end here. Integration with the larger society is the next and ongoing stage of coming out. Though we may want to stay safely in our communities, it is important to move beyond their confines to build bridges to others. Integration is being out in other communities besides our own.

It is not difference which immobilizes us, but silence. And there are so many silences to be broken.

Audre Lorde
writer

Each of us has a place in the struggle for freedom. Many gay brothers and sisters before us have laid the groundwork that makes it possible for us to be so much more visible than was possible just 20 years ago. Many of these pioneers were unrecognized but undauntedly fought discrimination and prejudice.

We must not become complacent with our current progress. Our work is not done. We must continue to stand up for ourselves and counter the upsurge in homo-hatred since we have become more visible, more affirming and more assertive.

Young lesbian and gay children need us to continue the fight so they can avoid some of the pain we have suffered. Previous generations have done so and so must we.

When one is a stranger to oneself the one is estranged from others too. If one is out of touch with oneself, then one cannot touch others.

Anne Morrow Lindbergh
writer

We are taught to reject our homosexuality. We become strangers unto ourselves. We live our lives for others and lose sight of who we are. We live our lives vicariously through the hopes and dreams of others.

Today, you do have the opportunity to reflect on who you are. Reclaim a part of you that has been estranged in order to please others. Put yourself first. Reclaim your homosexuality as a gift.

Of course I didn't have to talk about my sexual preference in public . . . Because of my homosexuality I can't get a job as a coach. Unless certain attitudes change there's no way for me to function in this society doing what I want to do. If some of us don't take on oppressive labels and publicly prove them wrong, we'll stay trapped by the stereotypes for the rest of our lives.

Dave Kopay
former professional football player

We must thank those lesbian and gay heroes who put their lives and careers on the line so that we might live in a more tolerant society. These individuals come from all walks of life. Many live remarkably "normal" lives. Yet the pain of the closet has propelled them to stand up and speak out against hatred and bigotry towards lesbians and gays. They became heroes by being true to themselves and standing up for what is right.

The ranks of heroes are growing: our community is filled with heroes who on a daily basis say no to homo-hatred.

We have forced gay people into the red-light districts, forced them to meet each other in bars and lurid places—then we call them promiscuous sinners.

Adele Starr
former president
Parents and Friends of Lesbians and Gays (PFLAG)

It's always easier to blame the victim than to identify the origins of the malice. It doesn't take much understanding to recognize that when you socialize individuals to hate themselves that there is greater tendency to act out a self-fulfilling prophecy of "I'm not okay."

It's refreshing to see heterosexual people (e.g., those parents involved in PFLAG) that recognize the victimization we have suffered. It is affirming to have family that speaks up for the injustices we endure.

As much as there are reasons to be critical of the heterosexual society we live in, we must not forget to show our appreciation to those who share our battles.

To assess the damage is a dangerous act.

Cherrie Moraga
writer

When we give ourselves permission to begin exploring how heterosexism has personally affected our being, we may respond with fear of confronting the pain or we may minimize the pain buried inside. When the pain seems overwhelming we may want to avoid it. However, breaking the silence and speaking about the pain is the first step in healing from cultural victimization.

Sharing our coming out stories, telling what it was like growing up lesbian or gay, is essential in our healing process. Too frequently we have grown up feeling isolated and alienated as positive images of lesbians and gays remain obscured. Sharing with supportive others heals our emotional wounds, and helps us realize we are not alone and we will survive.

Sharing our struggles is indeed a dangerous act for once we share we change our lives forever. There is no going back into the closet.

It seems like soon it will be weird to be heterosexual.

Harvard coed

In some circles it's fashionable to have lesbian and gay friends. On college campuses it is often seen as progressive, open-minded and a sign of "the new generation."

I believe lesbians and gays will gain even greater acceptance when this occurs in high schools across the country. As growing numbers of high school students accept lesbians and gays it will be seen as the right thing to do. Those teenagers accepting lesbians and gays will be the "in group" and will be on the cutting edge. This may be reinforced as part of "natural" adolescent rebellion against their parents rigidity and conformity, but as these adolescents grow up they will model tolerance and acceptance of lesbians and gays to their families and friends.

Heterosexuality is unlikely to become "weird," but it is clear that homosexuality is becoming more acceptable. Finally!

Cure Hate
Stop AIDS

Gay Men's Health Crisis (GMHC)

There are still too many people out there that view homosexuality as problematic and AIDS as a punishment for being homosexual. Let's put the focus where it really belongs: on the hate, on those people who spew their hate toward lesbians, gays and people with AIDS.

All forms of hatred need to be cured. All types of bigotry need to stopped. Remember, homosexuality is not a problem, hatred is. Join hands; help create a solution.

The suppressed lesbian I had been carrying in me since adolescence began to stretch her limbs.

Adrienne Rich
poet

Suppressing our homosexuality is a direct result of the years of socialization to hate and despise homosexuality. Deep within ourselves we know the truth. However, we are taught to deny the truth. Years may pass before we are able to allow ourselves to face our homosexuality. The severity of the victimization is related to the number of years of suppression.

Somehow we find the strength to acknowledge our homosexuality. Sometimes we have no choice. The inner voice screams so loudly that if we don't heed its call for release we are likely to self-destruct. What inner peace when we finally embrace that part of our being that society taught us to deny!

I have been perfectly happy the way I am. If my mother was responsible for it, I am grateful.

Christopher Isherwood
writer

Our gayness is a gift from our parents. What a wonderful gift to pass on to a child! Do these words sound strange? Let them resonate. Of course our gayness is a gift. Of course it is something beautiful.

Realizing this is made difficult only because of society's propensity to value one form of beauty over others, one gift over others. But how could one separate a gift that is part of the whole? Our gayness, just as our race and sex, is a gift and something of beauty because it is an integral part of who we are. And, it cannot be taken from any part of the whole.

Our gayness is a gift. Don't let others' ignorance keep you from recognizing it as one of your gifts.

If adjustment is necessary, it should be made primarily with regard to the position the homosexual occupies in present day society, and society should more often be treated than the homosexual.

Dr. Harry Benjamin
psychotherapist

Hear, hear! It is no longer homosexuality that is a problem. Rather the problem lies with those people who still hold prejudicial biases toward homosexuals. For years we have been told there's something wrong with us, but now we can clearly say there is something wrong with people who don't accept us.

Earlier in the twentieth century homosexuality was classified as a mental illness. It's now time to place the onus on those who will not accept anyone who is different from themselves. Unwillingness to accept and tolerate differences causes hatred throughout our world. This festering hatred is possibly the worst kind of sickness. The burden no longer lies on our shoulders.

Anita [Bryant], you are to Christianity what paint-by-numbers is to art!

Robin Tyler
entertainer

How many religious fundamentalists have a 1-2-3 approach to something they call salvation? Their insistence that they "know the way" for lesbians and gays when they are actually filled with hatred and know nothing about us is repulsive. This is yet another example of religious zealotry fueling hatred.

How many more conflicts and wars must our planet face before realizing that hatred based on religious beliefs is the antithesis of spirituality? Thankfully and with hope, lesbians and gays are reclaiming their spirituality for themselves, whether through religious institutions or personal journeys.

Our spirituality is embracing and nurturing. This is another way we teach the world how to love.

The books that the world calls immoral books are books that show the world its own shame.

Oscar Wilde
writer

Books banned or altered because of their homosexual or homoerotic content are clear examples of society's irrational fear and shame about homosexuality. Morality gets twisted into the likes and dislikes of the majority. Is it moral to silence a minority that is finally recognized by the educated as healthy, normal and posing no threat to society? Attempts to silence and control are the unrecognized but real immorality.

Breaking the silence that surrounds the prejudice we face as lesbians and gays not only helps each of us in our individual healing process, but also exposes the immorality of others.

To be civilized is to be incapable of giving unnecessary offense, it is to have some quality of consideration for all who cross our path.

Agnes Repplier

We demand tolerance and acceptance from the heterosexual community. This is not too much to ask. In fact, it is a rather basic demand and a necessity if we are to live as civilized people on this shrinking planet.

We need the same tolerance and acceptance we demand from heterosexuals when dealing with the diversity within the lesbian and gay community. Oppression breeds contempt, so that those who have been victimized learn to victimize others. Recognizing our participation in revictimizing members of our own community is the first step in building tolerance and acceptance within it.

Don't repeat the harmful stereotypes we grew up with. Reach out to someone different than yourself. If we expect heterosexuals to do so, we must do so ourselves.

[On "The Agony and the Ecstacy"]: *The movie stresses the love that blossomed between Michelangelo and Lorenzo the Magnificent's teenage daughter . . . this amorous relationship is more offensive to the knowledgeable spectator than the truth about Michelangelo's homosexuality.*

Life Magazine

Where is the chapter in history books about the contributions made by lesbians and gays? Refusing to acknowledge a historical figure's homosexuality is a grievous error. It leads to the underlying assumption that homosexuals have nothing to contribute to society.

Perpetuation of this myth is a frightening abuse of power by the education establishment. As lesbian and gay studies programs begin to develop at universities, we must also remember that primary and secondary school textbooks must acknowledge the homosexuality of Michelangelo, Gertrude Stein, James Baldwin and many others to help our children grow up free of hatred and bigotry.

343

....

Gay liberation should not be a license to be a perpetual adolescent. If you deny yourself commitment then what can you do with your life?

Harvey Fierstein
actor/playwright

When we come out of the closet after years of being forced to deny our sexuality, it is similar to re-experiencing adolescence—the adolescence we couldn't have in our teenage years. This can happen at any age and is often a time for us to revel in our homosexuality. This causes some heterosexuals to perpetuate stereotypes of us as immature, irresponsible and "adolescent," not realizing their part in delaying an important part of our development. Unfortunately, we may remain stuck in this adolescent "exploration" stage, thereby perpetuating a stereotype of irresponsibility.

Though this second adolescence is an essential part of our development, it is just one stage in our coming out process, not the be-all and end-all of what it means to be gay.

You're neither unnatural, nor abominable, nor mad; you're as much a part of what people call nature as anyone else; only you're unexplained as yet—you've not got your niche in creation.

Radclyffe Hall
author

People continue to try to "explain" us: they try to figure out how or why we're gay. The urge to explain, however, is decreasing as civilized people realize it is an irrelevant question. We're here, and we're not going away.

Some of the first gay and lesbian organizations, such as the Mattachine Society and the Daughters of Bilitis, maintained a level of secrecy to protect themselves. This is no longer necessary. There is every kind of lesbian and gay group including psychologists, athletic teams, political organizations, churches, etc.

We are creating and defining new communities reflecting our diversity. We no longer are limited, but have every opportunity to explore who we are as lesbian and gay individuals.

345

Ain't no way to read the bible and not think God white, she say. Then she sigh. When I found out I thought God was white, and a man, I lost interest.

Alice Walker
writer

We have often been told lesbians and gays cannot be spiritual. Look at the number of churches that in one way or another profess that God is reserved for heterosexuals or proclaim "hate the sin, love the sinner."

Many of us grow up questioning our capacity for spirituality as a result of these prejudicial messages. Healing from heterosexism involves reclaiming our spirituality. Our healing process provides an opportunity most heterosexuals do not have: we end up making very personal decisions about our spirituality instead of blindly following the religious traditions of our parents.

As we discover our spirituality, whether through activism or meditation, it becomes personal and meaningful. No one can deny us our spirituality when it flows from within.

346

I believe in a lively disrespect for most forms of authority.

Rita Mae Brown
author

As an oppressed minority we have had limited access to power. How can there be respect for those institutions that oppress us when they maintain their power and security at all costs, regardless of the harm inflicted on us?

Look at the military's attempts to continue the ban on lesbians and gays in the military. They state some people may be "uncomfortable" around gays and lesbians. Did it ever dawn on them to confront their own "uncomfortability?" Especially when we have lesbians and gays in the military with exemplary performance.

Of course there will be disrespect and contempt for those who continue to abuse their power. We will continue to speak up as long as injustice continues.

We always find ourselves in the position of having to play civil libertarian to a bunch of bigots who want their constitutional right to express their hatred of us.

Ronald Gold
journalist/gay activist

Freedom of speech? How far does it go until it becomes an abuse of power? To vilify and to shame is abusive. Lesbians and gays know the abusiveness of the hateful words others speak.

It's one thing to harbor feelings of contempt and hatred and privately express them. But to spew one's hatred on others is not a right, it's barbaric and fuels antagonistic behavior.

Point out the hate so others may see. Hate unveiled cannot thrive.

We use the pink and black triangles to remind us that all our lives and all our stories must never be forgotten if the atrocities of the past are to be never again.

Karen Peper

In Nazi concentration camps the inverted pink triangle was used to identify gay men and the inverted black triangle was forced upon many women, some identified as lesbians, others as prostitutes. Both are clear reminders of the oppression we face.

Lesbians and gays have reclaimed these symbols as a source of pride proclaiming "Never Again!" We must share our stories so the atrocities of the past are not forgotten nor repeated. "Never again!" is also a call to come out so history does not repeat itself.

Wear a pink or black triangle to show that lesbians and gays are everywhere, and we will not be forgotten or ignored.

You will never be rid of us because we produce ourselves out of your bodies.

Martha Shelley
writer

The "choice" we are faced with is not whether or not we are gay but whether or not we accept ourselves for who we are. We call this process "coming out," and we wouldn't struggle with it if we hadn't been raised in a heterosexist society. We wouldn't need to come out any more than heterosexuals need to "come out" as heterosexuals.

Coming out is best reframed as "healing from cultural victimization." Heterosexism, like other forms of cultural victimization, is a form of abuse that disempowers people. By reframing our process, we clearly recognize that we have been abused and we are not responsible for the abuse we have suffered.

The first step of healing from victimization involves recognizing the abuse that has occurred, and clearly identifying the perpetrators rather than blaming ourselves.

I ascertain that I'm homosexual. Okay that's no cause for alarm. How and why are idle questions. It's a little like wanting to know why my eyes are green.

Jean Genet
writer

Most attempts to determine the origins of homosexuality are based on the false premise that "there's something wrong with homosexuality and if we find the cause we can change it." Why not the same vigor in determining the origins of heterosexuality? Because homosexuality is feared and devalued, and the fearful and bigoted are obsessed with determining its origins.

We must remember that discovering the origins of homosexuality may help some people in their acceptance of homosexuality, but it really makes no difference what causes heterosexuality or homosexuality. When we value both, their beauty, rather than their origin, becomes the focus.

There's this illusion that homosexuals have sex and heterosexuals fall in love. That's completely untrue. Everybody wants to be loved.

Boy George
singer

How often have we been bombarded with the message that our relationships are based solely on sex! To focus only on the sexual nature of our relationships is a means to discredit our relationships, implying that they are not healthy, fulfilling, nurturing and loving. What could be so natural other than the love between two people regardless of their gender? It points to society's struggle to celebrate sexuality. Many people still cling to fearful, shaming messages about sexuality promulgated in the Middle Ages.

By loving each other we are teaching the world how to love. Release the shame society has instilled and let your love grow freely.

We turn not older with years, but newer every day.

Emily Dickinson
poet

Each day can bring something new. Each day can bring some rediscovery of our lesbian or gay self that has been hidden in our memory after so many years of hiding in the closet.

Discovering and rediscovering our lesbian and gay selves brings freshness, growth and maturity to our being. It also provides continual healing from the negative effects of heterosexism.

What hidden aspects of your lesbian or gay self remain uncovered? Celebrate how your gayness enriches every aspect of your life!

What is most beautiful in virile men is something feminine; what is most beautiful in feminine women is something masculine.

Susan Sontag
writer/critic

Society still promulgates rigid stereotypes by limiting masculinity to men and femininity to women. Lesbians and gays have challenged society to see that the feminine and masculine exist within both male and female. The fear and devaluation of the feminine is the root of sexism and heterosexism.

Beauty lies in embracing and celebrating all aspects of the self: both the femininity and masculinity of our being. Rejecting either aspect limits ourselves and perpetuates sexism and heterosexism.

We are leaders in destroying harmful, rigid stereotypes that limit self expression. As we celebrate our masculinity and femininity we encourage heterosexuals to wake up to their true selves!

Love him . . . love him and let him love you. Do you think anything else under heaven really matters?

James Baldwin
writer

Do not fear the love you have for others. We are told as children it is not natural or possible to fully love someone of the same sex, but love knows no bounds. Love is not based on gender. Loves comes from the heart and the soul. When love is stirred inside your being, follow it.

Too frequently we stifle the love we hold because of society's rigid messages about love. Unleash your love and let it happen. Love restrained lacks the passion love needs to be fulfilling. Love unleashed is powerful and bold. Let's have more love and less hate.

But it is not really difference the oppressor fears so much as similarity.

Cherrie Moraga
writer

Think about heterosexuality and homosexuality as universal components of sexuality, recognizing every individual with varying degrees of homosexual and heterosexual inclinations. Because we still live in a society that teaches us that any homosexual desire is wrong, we can better understand the fear some heterosexuals have of homosexuality, since it is their own homosexual proclivities they fear.

While lesbians and gays have done much to dispel the myths surrounding sexuality, there is still much to be learned. But once again, it's about understanding both how we're different and how we're the same.

[Introducing a federal gay rights bill]: *They are a very extensive minority who have suffered discrimination and who have the right to participation in the promise and the fruits of society as every other individual.*

Bella Abzug
former congresswoman

Although America represents freedom, many Americans continue to be oppressed, including homosexuals. How many years will it be before lesbians and gays will be free from the risk of loss of job, home or families due to irrational prejudices and discrimination?

Since the Stonewall riots positive change has occurred, including the enactment of legislation to protect lesbians and gays. Legislation is one part of the struggle to end discrimination: it is a significant reminder to heterosexual America that discrimination is wrong. To lesbians and gays it is a hope that our pain and suffering can subside.

Call or write a public official to help end discrimination. It does make a difference!

In an expanding universe, time is on the side of the outcast. Those who once inhabited the suburbs of human contempt find that without changing their address they eventually live in the metropolis.

Quentin Crisp
writer

In time society will accept homosexuality. Decades from now other generations will look with disbelief at the prejudicial and archaic treatment of lesbians and gays.

More accurate information about lesbians and gays is beginning to permeate society. Along with this, an increasing number of lesbian and gays are coming out to families and co-workers. As these trends continue, what was once considered aberrant, then tolerable, and to some even fashionable, will eventually be the familiar.

Friendship with oneself is all important, because without it one cannot be friends with anyone else in the world.

Eleanor Roosevelt

Self-acceptance and self-love are necessary in the development and maintenance of fulfilling friendships. Think of the times our struggle with accepting our homosexuality kept us distant from those people we desired more closeness with. When our lingering shame about our homosexuality kept us from being as open as we wanted to be with heterosexual friends and family. And even more demoralizing, when we limited our contact with our lesbian sisters and gay brothers because we still struggled with self-acceptance.

Each day we need to take steps to affirm our gayness. Befriending ourself opens the door for friendships.

Homosexuality for thousands of years has been the unnameable leprosy . . . For anyone to reach a level of self-esteem where one is actually proud of oneself . . . and able to see everything as God's creation, is what I would call tremendous.

Malcolm Boyd
Episcopal priest and gay activist

We are truly courageous and resilient persons. That so many of us are able to hold our heads high and proclaim loudly "Gay and Proud" is an act of courage.

As we celebrate our gayness we heal from society's abuses. The more we love ourselves, the less important society's response becomes.

When I feel good about myself, I realize that I can hold on to that self-love and that no one can take it away from me. Individuals may continue their shaming messages, but I refuse to let others' messages detract from my self-esteem.

I wasn't the most masculine child. The words "sissy" and "let's get him" were familiar to my ears . . . up in my room, I put on my own Broadway routines. I was the only person I knew who danced to the "I Love Lucy" theme.

Terry Sweeney
comedian

While the tauntings we endured as children prevented many of us from publicly expressing our real selves, within the walls of our own bedrooms our creativity, passion and dreams were given full reign. For some, the solace may have caused pain, but from that solace and suffering much life was born.

Those times when we savored the safety and comfort of our rooms were healing and empowering times for us. They protected us and helped us adapt to the cruel world outside our rooms. In those rooms the seeds of creativity were tended.

Today our talents and passions live on and are expressed openly and publicly. Take a look back at those childhood dreams.

He who wears his morality but as his best garment were better naked.

Kahlil Gibran
poet/artist

How many fundamental preachers have you heard about that spend all their time and energy "fighting the evils of homosexuality"? These preachers perpetuate and feed off the ignorance and hatred of their followers. Without the issue of homosexuality they would have nothing else to talk about and nothing else to offer their followers. Their careers are based on their hatred of homosexuals. Helping people realize this is essential in taking away the power of preachers who are abusing their power in the name of God.

We see through these preachers' false gods. We must continue to strip away their outer cloak of hatred so that all can see their true essence, and so that power is taken away from those who abuse their position.

Our feelings are our most genuine paths to knowledge.

Audre Lorde
writer

As children we intuitively know our attractions to others of the same sex are true and meaningful. However, we learn to discount what we know to be true under pressure to conform to heterosexuality. How often have we responded by trying to be heterosexual, hoping that if we could only force ourselves to be attracted to people of the opposite sex then we'd fit in, we'd be accepted and we'd be at peace with ourselves and our pain would subside?

It is often a long and painful road to return to what we knew to be true all along—that our same sex attractions are real—and that in spite of attempts by others to convince us this is unnatural, we know in our hearts it isn't.

We must learn to trust our feelings once again. Our feelings are the essence of our being.

Life shrinks or expands in proportion to one's courage.

Anaïs Nin
writer

Courage is a necessary part of moving from victim to survivor, of healing from heterosexism. Any steps we take to reclaim personal power (e.g., coming out, marching in a gay pride parade, calling our legislators to support gay rights, holding our partners' hands in public) are all acts of courage. And with each act, our courage increases. And as our courage increases we find endless possibilities of living in the world as proud lesbians and gays.

We are no longer confined to a life in the closet. As our courage expands, so does our life.

Gay culture is far from "marginal," being rather "intersectional," the conduits between unlike beings.

Judy Grahn
writer

While we are taught to believe lesbians and gays are unnecessary and unimportant in society, it is lesbian and gay people who are leading society from rigid and harmful sex role stereotypes to a more embracing and sane picture of what it means to be male and female. We are the courageous ones who have shown that maleness is not defined solely by masculinity, nor femaleness by femininity. Masculinity and femininity are essential parts of our being, regardless of our gender.

Celebrating both our masculinity and femininity offers the possibility for a deeper self-awareness. At the same time it helps break down harmful stereotypes that pit men against women and straights against gays. As we live our lives expressing both our masculinity and femininity, we teach others to explore those parts of the self they have not expressed.

There is a light in this world, a healing spirit more powerful than any darkness we may encounter. We sometimes lose sight of this force when there is suffering, too much pain. Then suddenly, the spirit will emerge through the lives of ordinary people who hear a call and answer in extraordinary ways.

Mother Teresa

When you reflect on the past year, how much light and how much darkness do you see? What pain have you suffered as a lesbian or gay person due to the prejudices we still face? What joy have you claimed because of your homosexuality?

Now, focus on the New Year. What will you do to bring more joy into your very own life? Keep hope alive. Hope fosters healing so that you can continue to reclaim pride.

ABOUT THE AUTHOR

Joseph H. Neisen received his Ph.D. from the Department of Family Social Science at the University of Minnesota. His work focused on the issues facing lesbians and gays, and their families of origin and families of choice. He has published numerous articles in the field and lectured nationally on his pioneering work re-examining heterosexism and homophobia.

Currently, Dr. Neisen is Program Director at Pride Institute in Minneapolis. Pride Institute is the nation's leader in providing alcohol and drug treatment services specifically for the lesbian, gay and bisexual community. In addition, he teaches several graduate courses in the Counseling Psychology Department at St. Mary's College of Minneapolis.